OCT

```
MEMORIAL MEDIA CENTER
1314648                B VEN
     Jesse Ventura
```

Jesse Ventura

by Michael V. Uschan

Lucent Books, San Diego, CA

Titles in the People in the News series include:

Garth Brooks
Sandra Bullock
George W. Bush
Jim Carrey
Tom Cruise
Bill Gates
John Grisham
Jesse Jackson
Michael Jackson
Michael Jordan
Stephen King
George Lucas
Dominique Moceanu
Rosie O'Donnell
Colin Powell
Princess Diana
Christopher Reeve
The Rolling Stones
Steven Spielberg
R. L. Stine
Jesse Ventura
Oprah Winfrey
Tiger Woods

No part of this book may be reproduced or used in any form or by any means, electrical, mechanical, or otherwise, including, but not limited to, photocopy, recording, or any information storage and retrieval system, without prior written permission from the publisher.

To Lev and Vivien DeBack, good friends and two of the most politically savvy people I know.

Library of Congress Cataloging-in-Publication Data

Uschan, Michael V., 1948–
  Jesse Ventura / by Michael V. Uschan.
    p. cm. — (People in the news)
  Includes bibliographical references and index.
  ISBN 1-56006-777-2 (alk. paper)
   1. Ventura, Jesse—Juvenile literature. 2. Governors—Minnesota—Biography—Juvenile literature. 3. Minnesota—Politics and government—1951—Juvenile literature. 4. Wrestlers—United States—Biography—Juvenile literature. [1. Ventura, Jesse. 2. Wrestlers. 3. Governors.] I. Title. II. People in the news (San Diego, Calif.)
  F610.3.V46 U83   2001
  977.6'053'092—dc21

00-010391

Copyright © 2001 by Lucent Books, Inc.
P.O. Box 289011
San Diego, CA 92198-9011
Printed in the U.S.A.

Table of Contents

Foreword	4
Introduction	
The Many Faces of Jesse Ventura	6
Chapter 1	
James George Janos	10
Chapter 2	
Janos "The Dirty"	22
Chapter 3	
Jesse "The Body" Ventura	34
Chapter 4	
Jesse "The Mouth" Ventura	47
Chapter 5	
Jesse "The Mayor" Ventura	59
Chapter 6	
Jesse "The Governor" Ventura	73
Epilogue	
Jesse "The President" Ventura?	89
Notes	94
Important Dates in the Life of Jesse Ventura	101
For Further Reading	103
Works Consulted	104
Index	107
Picture Credits	111
About the Author	112

Foreword

FAME AND CELEBRITY are alluring. People are drawn to those who walk in fame's spotlight, whether they are known for great accomplishments or for notorious deeds. The lives of the famous pique public interest and attract attention, perhaps because their experiences seem in some ways so different from, yet in other ways so similar to, our own.

Newspapers, magazines, and television regularly capitalize on this fascination with celebrity by running profiles of famous people. For example, television programs such as *Entertainment Tonight* devote all of their programming to stories about entertainment and entertainers. Magazines such as *People* fill their pages with stories of the private lives of famous people. Even newspapers, newsmagazines, and television news frequently delve into the lives of well-known personalities. Despite the number of articles and programs, few provide more than a superficial glimpse at their subjects.

Lucent's People in the News series offers young readers a deeper look into the lives of today's newsmakers, the influences that have shaped them, and the impact they have had in their fields of endeavor and on other people's lives. The subjects of the series hail from many disciplines and walks of life. They include authors, musicians, athletes, political leaders, entertainers, entrepreneurs, and others who have made a mark on modern life and who, in many cases, will continue to do so for years to come.

These biographies are more than factual chronicles. Each book emphasizes the contributions, accomplishments, or deeds that have brought fame or notoriety to the individual and shows how that person has influenced modern life. Authors portray their subjects in a realistic, unsentimental light. For example, Bill Gates—the cofounder and chief executive officer of the software giant Microsoft—has been instrumental in making personal computers the most vital tool of the modern age. Few dispute his business savvy, his perseverance, or his technical expertise, yet critics say he is ruthless in his dealings with competitors and driven more by his desire to maintain Microsoft's dominance in the computer industry than by an interest in furthering technology.

In these books, young readers will encounter inspiring stories about real people who achieved success despite enormous obstacles. Oprah Winfrey—the most powerful, most watched, and wealthiest woman on television today—spent the first six years of her life in the care of her grandparents while her unwed mother sought work and a better life elsewhere. Her adolescence was colored by promiscuity, pregnancy at age fourteen, rape, and sexual abuse.

Each author documents and supports his or her work with an array of primary and secondary source quotations taken from diaries, letters, speeches, and interviews. All quotes are footnoted to show readers exactly how and where biographers derive their information and provide guidance for further research. The quotations enliven the text by giving readers eyewitness views of the life and accomplishments of each person covered in the People in the News series.

In addition, each book in the series includes photographs, annotated bibliographies, timelines, and comprehensive indexes. For both the casual reader and the student researcher, the People in the News series offers insight into the lives of today's newsmakers—people who shape the way we live, work, and play in the modern age.

Introduction

The Many Faces of Jesse Ventura

JESSE VENTURA IS the only governor to ever end his inaugural speech with a cry of "Hooyah!" the signature phrase he learned as a member of the SEALs (SEa, Air, Land), the U.S. Navy's elite underwater commando corps. Ventura also is the first state chief executive who was a professional wrestler, a mouthy villain nicknamed "The Body" who wore pink tights and feathery boas as part of the exotic ring persona he had carefully crafted to become popular.

"We shocked the world. We really did,"[1] Ventura said January 4, 1999, when he was sworn in as Minnesota's thirty-eighth governor in St. Paul, the state capital. His victory November 3, 1998, had been so wildly unexpected that on election night, stunned CBS News television anchorman Dan Rather commented to the nation, "People could not be more surprised if Fidel Castro came loping across the Midwestern prairie on the back of a hippopotamus."[2]

Ventura's election was astounding because most people still equated him with his cartoonlike ring personality, which he had enacted for more than a decade. The fact that a member of the minor Reform Party had been able to defeat candidates of the more powerful Democratic and Republican parties was secondary to the unbelievable premise that a pro wrestler would now head a state that spent approximately $12 billion every two years to meet the needs of its citizens.

What most observers outside Minnesota failed to realize is that voters had not elected an ignorant, wild-eyed, hulking (the governor *is* six-feet-four-inches tall and weighs over 250 pounds) former grappler. The electorate had voted in a native son and former high school sports star, a Navy veteran who served in Vietnam, a devoted husband and father, a former mayor of the state's sixth-largest city, and an entrepreneur who developed a product—himself—and marketed it successfully to become rich.

Jesse Ventura or James Janos?

Jesse Ventura, the ring name he took when he became a wrestler, was born James George Janos on July 15, 1951, in Minneapolis, which shares with St. Paul the nickname of the "Twin Cities." The working class neighborhood Ventura grew up in is only a few miles from the governor's mansion in St. Paul, but Ventura traveled a long, twisting, sometimes bizarre career path to get there: Navy SEAL, war veteran, bodyguard for the Rolling Stones, nightclub bouncer, wrestler, sports announcer, actor, mayor, and radio talk show host.

Jesse Ventura takes the oath of office as Minnesota governor. From left to right behind him are his wife Terry, daughter Jade, and son Tyrel.

Before Ventura's election, most Americans knew him only from media images stemming from his highly public roles as a wrestler, actor, and announcer. The problem with trying to understand Ventura, however, is that he has always strictly separated his public and private lives: The feather-boaed crazy in the ring vanished when the match ended.

One way to gain a better understanding of this complex man is to study his inaugural speech on the day he was sworn in as governor. His words include references to his past that help provide a clearer, sharper image of the real Jesse Ventura.

Son, Father, Husband, Veteran

In a ten minute speech delivered without notes, Ventura mentioned how proud his parents, George Janos and Bernice Lenz Janos, would have been if they had lived to see him elected governor. He also noted, with his own share of pride, that his parents, World War II veterans, were both buried in a military cemetery:

> I want to thank my mother and father, who are there watching today at Fort Snelling National Cemetery. And I can tell right now that the ground's heating up a little bit where they're at. Because I think today, most of all, my mom and dad would look down and say, "I can't believe it. Look what he's done now."[3]

Ventura has never been shy about admitting he loved his parents and owes his success to the way they brought him up. Down-to-earth, hardworking people, they taught Ventura and his older brother, Jan, middle-class values that most people

On Veterans Day 1998, Governor-elect Jesse Ventura cleans up the gravesite of his parents, George and Bernice Janos, at Fort Snelling National Cemetery in Bloomington, Minnesota.

might suspect a pro wrestler lacked—patriotism, the need to work hard to achieve goals, the importance of family.

The new governor also thanked his own family for putting up with his quest to become governor. Again, it may surprise many that someone with such a gaudy public identity has been married for more than two decades to the same woman—he wed Teresa Masters in 1975—and is a loving family man:

> To my wife, Terry; my daughter, Jade; my son, Tyrel—they're riding along on another one of Dad's escapades, and we're not done yet. And I do owe them a thank you, because they're always there for me, no matter what it is I decide I'm going to try next, they're always there with full support, and they'll continue to be there, and I just hope that this doesn't change their lives too much, that they can go on being who they are and who I love them for.[4]

Another significant reference was his acknowledgment of his Navy friends who attended the inaugural. It is hard to reconcile the blowhard wrestler known as "The Body" with a war veteran who belonged to an elite military unit that demands discipline and self-sacrifice:

> I also want to thank my former teammates, many of who are here, and when I say teammates, yes, the United States Navy, [in] which I spent four glorious years of my life . . . the Navy teammates of mine sitting throughout the audience. It was a time in my life that created who I am today. It really and truly did.[5]

Not Quite an Angel

Those three roles—loving son, devoted family man, military veteran—are the ones Ventura has cherished most in his life. Like every human being, Ventura has character defects, including a giant-sized ego that at times equals that of his ring persona, "The Body," that have led him to make mistakes. But the man who became Minnesota's governor is a much more complex, interesting, and capable person than the loudmouthed braggart who wrestled Hulk Hogan and had his own action figure.

Chapter 1

James George Janos

At some point during elementary school, every child is asked what he or she wants to be when they grow up. It happened to James "Jim" Janos when he was nine and attending Cooper Elementary School on the south side of Minneapolis. Jim and his older brother, Jan, loved to listen to radio broadcasts of wrestling shows, which were popular in the Midwest. When the inevitable question came, Jim said he wanted to be a wrestler. Steve Nelson, one of his closest childhood friends, remembers that fateful day:

> Typically when you're in grade school you have a career day and tell people what you want to do. Jim got up there and said he wanted to be a professional wrestler. The teacher said, "That's a ridiculous idea. Go sit down. Who would want to be a professional wrestler?"[6]

If he had picked a far loftier goal, perhaps becoming governor of Minnesota, the teacher might have been more positive about his career choice. It is doubtful, however, that the teacher would have been any more confident that Jim could be elected governor than ever gain fame as a wrestler. Yet somehow, this young boy from a working-class family would achieve both those unlikely career choices. And his parents are due much of the credit for Ventura's success.

His Parents

The section of the Minnesota governor's Internet site that gives personal details of his life refers to Ventura's mother and father as "Sgt. George Janos" and "First Lt. Bernice Janos." The use of military designations for his parents, who were civilians by the time he was born, shows how deeply their service during World War II impressed him. His mother was a U.S. Army nurse and his father fought in the infantry under legendary General George Patton.

The military ranks also indicate how zealously Ventura safeguards their memories. In fact, while he was watching NBC's *Jesse Ventura*, a 1999 biography of his life, he turned off the made-for-television movie because he did not like the way his parents were being portrayed:

> First of all, my father was a very fun-loving, happy man; this guy wasn't that at all. My mother was, before it was even popular in the women's lib movement, a career woman and Army lieutenant who was aggressive and career-oriented and taught me and my brother to be independent thinkers and doers. Neither of these people were anything close to what my parents were like.[7]

During World War II, Jesse Ventura's parents, Sgt. George Janos and First Lt. Bernice Lenz, both served in North Africa. In this picture, the First Army marches through Tunisia on the African front in 1943.

Bernice Lenz was born in 1918 and grew up on a farm near Independence, Iowa. She defied society's expectations of young women in that era by leaving her rural home and moving to a big city to pursue her goal of a medical career. In 1940, after graduating from nursing school at Milwaukee Lutheran Hospital, she enlisted in the Army and soon became a first lieutenant serving in Europe and North Africa.

George Janos had been born in Pennsylvania in 1908 to immigrants from Czechoslovakia. His father worked in the coal mines but later moved to Minneapolis in search of a better life because mining, one of the few jobs open to immigrants in Pennsylvania, was such a hard, dangerous occupation. Janos only attended school through the eighth grade, but he was a hard worker. He also was deeply patriotic. When the United States entered World War II in December 1941 after the Japanese attack on Pearl Harbor, he enlisted in the Army even though he was thirty-two years old, the maximum age for acceptance into the military. If Janos had not enlisted, he might have avoided having to fight for his country, because he would have been too old for service by the time the military could have drafted him.

A member of a tank-destroyer crew, Janos fought in North Africa, Italy, and elsewhere in Europe, earning seven medals for bravery. He never talked about his battlefield exploits, a trait his son would adopt after serving in the Navy, but when Jim was a young boy he saw historic film of his father marching with other soldiers during a television documentary about World War II. In 1999, Ventura wrote:

> I was not the first member of my family to appear on television—dad made it well before I did. There was a showing on a Sunday night, and my entire family were gathered around the TV watching it. The big story that night was the battle at the Remagen Bridge. Suddenly there was my dad up on the screen crossing the bridge with the other GIs. We knew it was him because almost immediately afterwards, the phone rang and it was my mom's parents out in Iowa. "Were you watching," they asked. "We saw George crossing the Remagen Bridge."[8]

Ventura's parents did not meet until 1945, when his father returned home after the war and his mother moved to Minneapolis to study to become a nurse anesthetist. The match was an unlikely pairing: George was in his late thirties, a decade older, had far less education, and during the war was an enlisted man while his wife had been an officer. They fell in love anyway and were married a year later, but Ventura said his mom and dad never totally forgot the gap in their respective military ranks:

> My dad was a sergeant, so whenever they had a fight when I was a kid, that fact came out. Dad would always call my mom "the lieutenant," which would irritate my mother no end. Something about the standard story that enlisted men would always blame the officers just because they were officers.[9]

A Quiet War Hero

Jesse Ventura has always been proud of his father's record of valor in World War II, but he never knew the extent of his heroism until after his dad died, because George Janos never talked about the many battles he fought. When Britt Robson interviewed Ventura in 1998 for the Minneapolis newspaper *City Pages*, the candidate for governor became very emotional—"his eyes filled with tears," Robson wrote—when he talked about the emotional scars his dad carried from the war:

> My father had seven bronze battle stars in World War II that I never learned about until after he died at age 83. I was with him for 39 years of my life and I never had any idea that this man had seven bronze battle stars. You know how I learned it? My father's [discharge record] was shrunk down in his wallet and I took a magnifying glass and read it. My mother, who was a nurse in North Africa in the war, told me something later about my father that I never. . . . It had to do with the fact that in all the 39 years that I knew my dad, he never drove a car. He had a license, but he never drove. My mother drove. And my father's explanation to me was he didn't trust himself, which I accepted. I found out later why. And to be blunt, it's nobody else's business why. And if you'll excuse me a minute, it tears me up when I think about why. Because it dealt with the war, and therefore it's no one's business.

George Janos worked as a maintenance worker and steamfitter for the city of Minneapolis and his wife was a nurse. The Janos family was well provided for economically and it was the lieutenant who controlled the purse strings and invested the family savings. "She played the stock market and she was good at it," Terry Ventura said of her mother-in-law. "She would salt money away and juggle accounts and never buy anything on credit."[10]

Bernice's desire to pay in cash for every purchase, even a new car, was a trait shared by many other men and women of her generation. After struggling through the economic hard times of the Great Depression in the 1930s, many people remained cautious in their spending habits and fearful of future financial problems for the rest of their lives. Once, however, George strayed from his wife's strict financial discipline, taking money she was saving for a car and using it to buy some lakeside property so the family could have a summer vacation home. The incident occurred when Jim was about seven, and he and his brother waited for their mother to explode in anger when she found out what had happened. Instead, she calmly said, "Well, we'll just have to make do with the old car for a while."[11]

A Fun-Filled Childhood

Jim grew up in a loving household and enjoyed a happy childhood. He, his brother, and their many friends engaged in a variety of athletic competitions, including wrestling matches that Jim staged:

> The Saturday-afternoon fights—sixth-grade style. I'd put together a makeshift "ring" in my parents' basement, then I'd match up different combinations of my classmates. I set the fights up, refereed them, and went head-to-head in more than a few of them myself. This was just the kind of thing you did for fun if you were a kid growing up on the South Side of Minneapolis, Minnesota.[12]

Jim and Jan spent a lot of time outdoors playing a wide variety of sports, fishing, hunting, and swimming in both the

James George Janos   15

Rush hour traffic pours into Jesse Ventura's hometown of Minneapolis, which shares with neighboring St. Paul, Minnesota's state capital, the nickname of the "Twin Cities."

Mississippi River, which runs through Minneapolis, and at the lake where their dad had bought property behind their mother's back. Jim was popular and had a lot of friends, including Tom Delano, Kevin Johnson, Ricky Bjornson, and Jerry Flatgard, buddies who meant so much to him that he stayed in touch with most of them even after he became a famous wrestler and then governor of Minnesota.

Although Jim and Jan loved doing things together and had a good relationship, they weren't very much alike. In *Body Slam: The Jesse Ventura Story*, Ventura biographer Jake Tapper notes that they had contrasting personalities:

> They were very different in temperament. Jan was hard working, quiet, reserved. His room was immaculate. He was intense and introspective. However much he looked up to his brother, Jim was his opposite. He was a mischievous scamp, always getting into trouble. He was a slob and didn't work very hard in school.[13]

But even though Jim was not much of a student, his parents saw to it that he attended school every day and was well behaved in the classroom. Delano, one of Jim's best friends growing up, remembers that "[Jim] had rules to live by. He arrived promptly at the school. He was not absent at all. He was very well mannered."[14] Ventura believes that one of the most important lessons he learned from his parents was to be self-sufficient. "My parents taught my brother and me to be very independent and self-reliant," Ventura said. "Don't count on other people. Do it yourself."[15]

A Star Athlete

Although as an adult he would perform as a wrestler and actor, experiences that would later make it easier for him to give speeches and make public appearances as a political candidate and elected official, Jim was a shy young boy when he began attending Sanford Middle School. But at Sanford he first learned to wrestle, and his success in athletics helped boost his confidence and make him more outgoing. Writes biographer Tapper:

> Jim loved the sport [of wrestling], knew the holds and moves and surprised his fellow grade-school opponents whenever his gym class would pair off and wrestle. An average student, the sleepy-eyed, slightly goofy-looking kid would come alive in athletics.[16]

When Jim began attending Roosevelt High School in 1966, Jan, who also was an excellent athlete, was captain of the school's swimming team. The brothers had grown up playing in the strong currents of the Mississippi and both were excellent swimmers. Jim joined his brother on the swim team and as a senior in 1969 was named captain, leading the team to a 6-3 record. Jim also was the first high school athlete in Minneapolis to swim the 100-yard butterfly in under one minute. The butterfly stroke is the hardest in swimming, demanding strength and stamina as much as excellent technique, and the hard-muscled Jim was perfectly suited to excel at such a difficult event.

Jim also played football for the Teddys—the nickname stems from the school's namesake, President Theodore Roosevelt—and

James George Janos

James George Janos (later to become Jesse Ventura), in his senior class photo taken in 1969.

became one of Roosevelt's most popular students. When Jim graduated in 1969, the yearbook showed a tall, slim, short-haired young athlete, muscular but still lean at six-feet-two-inches and 190 pounds. He was voted the title of "Best Physique" and the yearbook includes a comical picture of Jim posing next to Kathy Buck, a pretty blonde who was voted "Best Figure"; Jim is gripping two small hand weights while Buck, wearing a dress suit, is holding a much heavier looking barbell. Even as a teenager, he had a highly developed sense of humor, one that he did not mind occasionally turning on himself.

Ventura has told his son, Tyrel, about the fun and friends he had in high school. "My dad was just Mister Popularity. Everyone at Roosevelt knew my dad," Tyrel has said. But Ventura's son also knows that as a teenager his dad "was a rowdy kid. He told me about a lot of stuff they did, messing around in high school, throwing kids in lockers, things like that. He was a little bit of a troublemaker."[17]

His Wild Youth

Jim Janos was no angel while growing up. He engaged in most of the usual coming-of-age activities that attract teenagers, some of them illegal, such as drinking alcohol. "I was mischievous," Ventura admits. "Put it this way . . . I thank a higher being that my son wasn't me. And I feel bad for my mom and dad, because I caused way more problems than my son has ever caused me."[18]

For example, when Jim was in sixth grade he and his friends would sleep outside in tents in someone's backyard. But as soon as their parents went to bed, the boys would leave and roam the neighborhood, having fun and staying out until 2 A.M. or 3 A.M. The boys would even stuff clothes in their sleeping bags so it would look like they were still there if their parents checked on them.

In *I Ain't Got Time to Bleed*, which Ventura wrote after he became governor, he is unusually open for an elected official about some of the wild things he did when he was young. Actors and other celebrities can get away with being honest about some of the stupid, even illegal, stunts they pulled while growing up, but politicians usually try to conceal or minimize their involvement in such youthful escapades. Not Ventura, who says he and the "South Side Boys" he palled around with began drinking even before they entered high school:

> We were adventurers. We roamed the [Mississippi] riverbank. And we drank. In that era, that's what you did. This was early junior high school. We'd go down to the sandbar on the Mississippi riverbank on Saturday and Sunday mornings, because the older kids always had beer parties on Friday and Saturday nights. If you went down there early the next morning, you could always find a few beers lying in the sand, ones they'd lost during the night. We had a little cave where we hid them. Then when we accumulated about thirty of them, on a Saturday we'd tell our families we were going to the river all day.[19]

The teenage pranks the future governor was involved in included making an effigy of a teacher he and his friends disliked and hanging it from the flagpole at Sanford Middle School;

fighting with tough kids who were in gangs, even though Ventura claims he and his friends never belonged to a gang; and illegally buying beer when he was only sixteen. "We weren't juvenile delinquents," Ventura states. "I wouldn't put it that way. We just had a streak of mischief in us. And if one of us dared the other to do something, it would happen."[20]

Early Political Awakening

He put far more energy into excelling in athletics than in his school work, something Ventura now says he regrets because of the lost opportunity to learn more. But he wasn't dumb. "Contrary to what some people thought, he was a very sharp individual,"[21] remembers Freeman "Mac" McInroy, an assistant football coach and Ventura's eleventh-grade history teacher. McInroy said Jim excelled in his class because he was interested in politics and current affairs, had strong opinions on just about every subject, and loved to engage in heated debates about the merits of various issues.

Friendship Is Important to Jim Janos/ Jesse Ventura

When Jim Janos was growing up, he had a lot of good friends. Amazingly, most of the members of the small group he calls "the South Side Boys" have remained in touch with Jim through his name change to Jesse Ventura and wild climb to fame as a wrestler and then governor of Minnesota. In *I Ain't Got Time to Bleed*, Ventura writes that he is grateful to his friends for helping him keep a perspective on his life:

> You can't get a good sense of what's at the core of who I am until I tell you about the South Side Boys. We were the 1960s version of the Little Rascals. They're lifelong friends. I know no matter what I do in life, they're there to bring me back to reality. They're my reality check. They know me as Jim Janos, the kid down the block who grew up with them. And I'll always be him. I always remember that power can corrupt, so that's one of the reasons I'm thankful for the South Side Boys. They would never let me get too far out of line. They've done so much to keep me focused on who I am. I have them to thank for giving me such a solid base to push off into life from. It makes it a lot easier to put yourself out there when you know you've got lifelong friends at home that you can always come back to.

McInroy said at one point Jim became passionate about doing something to stop a growing problem with litter that was damaging Lake Nokomis, a local recreational spot. Although most people in the late 1960s were only just starting to become concerned about environmental issues, Ventura took a strong conservationist stand on the future of the lake. "We've got to protect things," McInroy remembers Jim saying. "We can't have it messed around."[22]

His early interest in politics was ignited by his parents, who both closely followed what was happening in government and

A Political Lesson

The Vietnam War divided many families in the 1960s. Although George Janos was a World War II veteran, he opposed the war while his son backed it. In a story in *George* magazine, Ventura recalled the debates he had with his father about the conflict and his dad's cynicism for elected officials:

> Another important early lesson from home was a distrust of the establishment. "My father was pretty negative on politicians," Ventura recalls. "His term for Nixon was 'the tailless rat.'" Childhood friend Steve Nelson remembers visiting and hearing George shouting: "He would rant and rave about politicians and how crooked they were. You'd hear him in the background, and Jim would say something like 'Oh, some politician has got him irritated again.'" In high school, Ventura began challenging authority—his father's, especially on the subject of the Vietnam War. "I would come home and try to sell him on the fact that we were there to stop the communists and the domino effect, which we were being taught in school. . . . My father said, 'Domino effect? This has nothing to do with stopping the communists! Somebody's getting rich.' [Today] I think he was right."

Although many young people in 1969 protested the Vietnam War or refused to serve in the armed forces, James Janos supported the war.

had strong opinions on many subjects. His father was especially vocal. Ventura, who admits he is as stubborn as his parents, loved to argue with his father about political issues, including the Vietnam War, which he supported and his dad opposed. "He and his father used to debate politics and religion all the time," said Terry Ventura. "When it seemed like they were at the worst with each other, they were actually having the time of their life."[23]

His Brother's Footsteps

Like many young boys, Jim felt fortunate to have an older brother he could pal around with and learn from. Even today, after Ventura has accomplished so much, he still deeply admires his brother, Jan:

> He was the opposite [in personality], he is very quiet and very to himself. He is the type of person who can't speak in front of 30 people; that would terrify him to death. And yet he can go off and run a marathon and think nothing of it. In his own way he is stronger than I am. And he joined the SEALs before I did. . . . And that was how I made it through training—how could I come home, and my parents would say, "Gee, well, Jan made it and you didn't."[24]

Jim admired his brother so much that he followed him into the Navy and the greatest real adventure of his life. Like Jan, he would become a SEAL.

Chapter 2

Janos "The Dirty"

THREE FACTORS INFLUENCED Jim Janos to join the elite Navy SEALs (SEa, Air, Land)—his brother, a popular war film, and a small plastic toy the Janos boys played with as children. The most important was the example set by his brother, who was three years older than Jim and became a SEAL first. Although the two had very different personalities, Ventura has often acknowledged the powerful influence Jan wielded over him while they were growing up:

> When you have an older brother, you tend to follow him in everything he does. He became an athlete; I became an athlete. He got into swimming; I got into swimming. He became a swimming captain; I became a swimming captain. And then later he became a SEAL. It wasn't until after the service that Jan and I started to go off on different paths.[25]

Swimming came naturally to the Janos boys and in high school they learned to dive using scuba (self-contained-underwater-breathing-apparatus) gear; it was a skill that would play an important part in their work when they became SEALs. Jim also says he and Jan became fascinated at an early age with becoming underwater warriors:

> Like so many of our generation, we had learned about [the SEALs] from the Richard Widmark movie *The Frogmen*. It seemed like a natural thing for us to gravitate to the [SEALs] in the service. It wasn't just that Widmark movie. When we were little kids, my mom had bought

the two of us these little plastic frogmen that swam in the water. Swimming might be too big a word for what they did. You filled up part of this little plastic man with baking soda, and he would rise and fall in the water as the soda fizzed into bubbles. That was Jan's favorite toy when he was a kid, and it stuck with him for years.[26]

The two young boys who played with that cheap plastic toy and avidly watched the melodramatic war movie did not realize it, but their activities were good practice for the lives they would one day lead. Both would become Navy frogmen and engage in underwater military operations during the Vietnam War.

Joining the Navy

During Christmas vacation in 1968, when Jim was a high school senior, his brother came home on leave after serving a tour of duty with the SEALs in Da Nang, in what was then South Vietnam. Tanned, fit, and with the aura of a soldier just returned from war, Jan was a heroic figure to Jim and to one of Jim's best friends, Steve

Richard Widmark (right), starred in The Frogmen. *The movie about undersea heroics during World War II helped inspire Jesse Ventura to become a Navy SEAL.*

Nelson. The stories Jan told of what he had gone through personally, from the challenge of SEAL training to actual combat, seemed adventurous and romantic to the teenage boys.

Jan, however, tried to persuade them not to follow in his path. "Don't go in," he advised them. "Go to college. Just go to college and have fun."[27] That's what Jim had planned to do until he failed to win a swimming scholarship to Northern Illinois University. Even though Jim had taken the required college-prep courses, such as advanced algebra, physics, and chemistry, his grades were not good enough to meet the school's academic standards. And if Jim couldn't swim competitively, he didn't see any reason to go to college, a decision that was disappointing to George and Bernice Janos, who had wanted both their sons to get a good education.

After graduating in the spring of 1969 from Roosevelt High School, Jim went to work for the state highway department. But his buddy "Nelse" couldn't purge the exotic images Jan had created in

Navy SEALs History

In *The Teams: An Oral History of the U.S. Navy SEALs*, authors Kevin Dockery and Bill Fawcett explore the history of this elite military unit by focusing on the experiences of individual SEALs, including Jim Janos. In a foreword, the authors explain the SEAL mission and how the units were created:

> SEAL teams today are trained to conduct a wide variety of missions. These missions can include observation and target designation, counter-terrorism, hostage rescue, Combat Search and Rescue (CSAR), and Visit, Board, Search, and Seizure (VBSS) operations. All SEALs today are the inheritors of the reputation earned by SEAL Teams One and Two in the jungles and swamps of Vietnam during the 1960s and early 1970s. [President] John Fitzgerald Kennedy had served with the PT squadrons of World War II and knew personally what a highly trained unit of men could do in taking unconventional warfare to the enemy. Following his own knowledge and the recommendations of his advisors, President Kennedy directed all of the services to create unconventional warfare units. None of the services took the president's direction with any more enthusiasm than his own Navy. The SEAL teams were first commissioned in January 1962 by [President Kennedy].

his mind. Nelson decided he wanted to become a SEAL and asked Jim to go with him to the Navy recruiting office. "I wanted him to go down with me," Nelson said years later. "He said, 'Now you remember, we're not going to enlist.' I said, 'I know, I just want to go down and talk to them.'"[28]

The two young men visited the recruitment center September 11. Ventura later said it was like going to a car dealership and being talked into buying an automobile he did not want. What he "purchased" was a six-year Navy enlistment, with the promise that he would be considered for SEAL training. Deep down, Jim had probably wanted to follow Jan into the Navy all along. He had felt angry and betrayed all summer after losing the scholarship. He sensed that he was drifting through life, so why not do something adventurous?

The two recruits had 120 days until they had to report for induction into the Navy, so Jim went back to work, but only long enough to earn money to last him until he had to enter the service. When he had saved enough, Jim quit to concentrate on spending his small horde of cash and having a good time in his final weeks as a civilian.

On January 5, 1970, Janos and Nelson departed for Coronado Naval Amphibious Base in San Diego, California. The SEAL training that followed his initial basic training would be the most difficult, demanding, hellish experience of his life.

Becoming a SEAL

The boot camp that introduced him to military life was no problem for the athletic, muscular Janos, but he almost didn't become a SEAL because he is color-blind. He failed the initial test but passed the second time, when a SEAL who knew his brother administered the eye exam and forged medical documents to show Janos had successfully identified various colors. Years later Ventura wrote how grateful he was for his chance to become a SEAL and how the tester's act symbolized the esprit d' corps of the SEALs, who operate in units called Teams: "To me [the tester's] actions were the essence of what being in the Teams was all about. In the Teams, it wasn't what you said that mattered, it was what you did and who you were as an individual. I deserved at least a chance, and they gave it to me."[29] It is a philosophy that still guides his life today.

After boot camp, Janos went to a specialty school to learn to be a storekeeper. Even though he wanted to be a SEAL, he had to know how to do a Navy job so he could be given a rank. And SEAL training is the most difficult in any branch of the military, with many failing to finish; if he washed out of the program, Janos would have to start doing the job he had been trained for. In a *U.S. News & World Report* article about the Special Operation Forces, such as the Green Berets and Army Rangers, Richard J. Newman and Rick Rickman describe the torturous SEAL training:

> SEAL applicants are immersed in frigid water until they are nearly hypothermic, knocked dizzy as they slog through crashing surf, and forced to carry muscle-melting rubber rafts over their heads every time they jog from place to place. Hell Week, which comes in the fifth week of training, brings an additional challenge—barely any sleep for five nights. Such tests eliminate up to 70 percent of trainees, a dropout rate similar to that of other special-operations branches.[30]

The six months of Basic Underwater Demolition/SEAL (BUD/S) Training is designed to simulate a combat environment and test the recruits' desire to complete the course. Janos was in Class 58 while Nelson, whose specialty schooling took longer, entered Class 59. SEAL training starts with six weeks of intense physical conditioning, military maneuvers, and other tasks that continually push candidates to the brink of physical, mental, and emotional breakdown.

The finale of Phase One, called Motivation Week by the instructors and Hell Week by recruits is a stretch from Sunday through Friday that increases the demands on recruits to simulate the rigors of combat, when the enemy might not allow them a chance to rest. "That's what separates the men from the boys," Ventura says. "Hell Week eliminates the bananas. A banana is

Janos "The Dirty"

A Navy SEAL carries a buddy during an exercise at the Coronado Naval Amphibious Base in San Diego, California. Surviving SEAL training was one of the most grueling ordeals Jesse Ventura ever had to endure.

someone who is soft on the inside and soft on the outside, and he's out of there pretty fast."[31]

Two things helped Janos survive SEAL training: his physique, which enabled him to meet the physical challenges, and the fear of failing in a situation in which his older brother had succeeded. But he admits it was not easy:

> I think back on it today and think, How did I do it? It was 22 weeks of—you run everywhere. You are not allowed to walk; at every point during the day, you have to be double-timing it. All your runs are done in combat boots in the sand, usually soaking wet—they usually run you into the ocean first and then you run wet and dry out. [He laughs at that.] I was never the same after that. Because then you truly know who you are down inside.[32]

After surviving Hell Week, Janos advanced to demolition and land warfare training, and then a third phase that focused on underwater diving. After completing basic SEAL training in November 1970, Ventura went to several other specialty schools. He learned to parachute, studied SERE (Survival, Escape, Resistance and Evasion) techniques he would use if he became

A Near-Death Experience During Training

SEAL training is dangerous as well as difficult, with many candidates becoming seriously injured or facing life-threatening situations. It was at SEAL Cadre school that Jim Janos almost died. During a training mission to destroy two bridges, Janos nearly drowned when the boat carrying him and several other SEALs overturned in a river after going over a small dam. He related the near-death experience in *The Teams: An Oral History of the U.S. Navy SEALs*:

> Sinking deeper, it was like I had climbed into a washing machine. The turbulence of the water tossed me around and I was completely disoriented. There was no way I knew which direction up was. And my breath was running out. Just as suddenly as I had entered it, the water tossed me to the surface [but] the water immediately sucked me back down as quickly as it had spit me up. There hadn't been a chance for me to blow and get a fresh lungful of air. Back into the washing machine I went, tumbling around again. . . . I was going to die and there wasn't much I could do about it. . . . My lungs were burning and I had no idea how long I had been under water. I did see my mom and dad looking down at me, I spoke but they couldn't hear me and could only cry. Just as I was going to become another statistic, my head popped above water and I was able to exhale and get two quick breaths of air. As I started to hold my breath again, my boots dragged the bottom and I was able to stand up slightly. From that day forward, I became a firm believer in fate. To this day, I believe there is a certain day that you are fated to die, and there isn't anything you can do about it. And that day on the river wasn't my time.

Navy SEALs learn to dive into the water from speeding boats. Techniques like these are difficult to master and can be dangerous if done incorrectly.

a prisoner of war, and took classes in guerrilla warfare at SEAL Cadre school. Shortly after completing training Jim Janos, storekeeper third class, was on his way overseas.

Overseas Duty

Janos, one of only forty to survive SEAL training from an original class of 125, was assigned to the Navy's command center in Subic Bay in the Philippine Islands as a member of Underwater Demolition Team (UDT) 12. It was there that he was given a new nickname by Lieutenant Commander Bruce Dyer, who knew his brother. Jim became "Janos the Dirty" while Jan was "Janos the Clean" because of the way they maintained their lockers and personal possessions. Jim wasn't very meticulous about how he kept his things; for example, he didn't like polishing his boots or starching his uniform. One reason he loved being deployed to a foreign country was that discipline was not as strict:

> Being overseas was the best part of being in the Teams, and I loved every minute of it. You had a direct mission to do and no one barked on [you] about stupid stuff. Things like your boots being polished weren't as important on deployment as the operating you had to do. Normal working uniform was cammies [camouflage] fatigues when you weren't wearing swim trunks and blue-and-golds [T-shirts].[33]

His first tour was a standard six months, but Janos enjoyed it so much that he volunteered to stay on three more months. SEAL teams were dispatched from Subic Bay to problem areas in Vietnam and other countries on a variety of missions Ventura has always declined to talk about. "Military is a personal thing," the former SEAL states. "It's however you choose to handle it when you're done, and it's no one's business but yours. I was ordered by my commanding office not to discuss anything because of the nature of work the SEALs [do]."[34]

However, he has acknowledged that most of his missions involved demolition work and that his assignments carried him to Vietnam, Hong Kong, Korea, Thailand, Okinawa, and Guam.

While in Vietnam, Janos made more than 100 parachute jumps and dived as deep as 212 feet, often in shark-infested waters. In *The Teams: An Oral History of the U.S. Navy SEALS*, authors Kevin Dockery and Bill Fawcett discuss the type of missions SEALs performed during the Vietnam War:

> Platoons of ten men and two officers, later expanded to twelve men and two officers, performed operations that had never been conducted by U.S. forces before. Using the many waterways of Southeast Asia as their means of [travel to and from their targets], small units of SEALs took the Viet Cong's methods of guerrilla warfare back to the enemy themselves. SEALs would spend long hours crouching in the dark waters of Vietnam, sometimes with only their heads showing, waiting to trigger an ambush on VC boats moving through canals and streams. Terrifying minutes were also experienced by SEALs conducting audacious prisoner snatch operations in broad daylight deep in enemy territory.[35]

Janos's second deployment overseas also was to Subic Bay, but because the Vietnam War was winding down, he had more spare time. While not involved in training or other duties, he played football and his team won the All-Service Championship by beating squads from the Army, Navy, Marines, and Air Force. Janos, who during this period began bulking up by weight lifting, was a defensive lineman who sacked a lot of opposing quarterbacks. His second tour of duty overseas was eight months, giving him a total of seventeen months of foreign service.

Dyer, his executive officer from 1971 through 1973, remembers Janos as a good though unspectacular sailor. "He was just another one of the 125 enlisted men," Dyer said. "I don't think he really stood out except for his size and his large personality. He was just an average-to-good Navy frogman."[36]

Fun and Games Overseas

The SEALs worked hard—even when they didn't have a military assignment, their physical training was demanding enough

Navy SEALs have to learn how to fight on land as well as in the water. These SEALs are in training at the Coronado Naval Amphibious Base in San Diego, California.

to test the stamina of a trained athlete—but they also partied hard. In *I Ain't Got Time to Bleed*, Ventura boasts of his carousing overseas, where he was treated as an adult even though he was in his teens:

> I loved the Philippines. I was stationed at Subic, and I loved going into Olongapo [a small town near the base]. It was more like the Wild West than any other place on Earth. In Olongapo, there's a one-mile stretch of road that has 350 bars. . . . At various bars you had your pick of rock 'n roll, country and western, you name it. It was a decadent city. To the kid I was then, it was paradise.[37]

The drinking, fights, and other wild times Ventura elaborates on in his book are not much different from the coming of age exploits of most teenagers when they begin testing the boundaries of their new freedom their first time away from home. "Part of the military life was social drinking—like on a college campus," says Paul Spark, who served with him overseas. "We did have parties—you were living for the moment; there was a war on."[38]

But Spark maintains that when Janos was on duty, he performed professionally and did his job like the rest of the SEALs.

His SEAL Legacy

Despite the party atmosphere that is a big part of the military lifestyle, young men and women who serve in the armed forces usually absorb important lessons that can help them the rest of their life: self-discipline, being responsible for assigned duties, and the need to work as a team to get things done. Ventura says that what he learned when he was a SEAL influences him today. During his campaign for governor of Minnesota, Ventura was asked by a reporter for *City Pages* magazine whether being a SEAL had helped him grow up or had changed his personality. The reporter, Britt Robson, noted that the usually animated, excitable gubernatorial candidate was very subdued in responding to the first two questions on the subject:

> ### Pain and "Flappers"
>
> SEAL training is perhaps the most brutal, stressful, and physically demanding training of any branch of the U.S. military. It didn't take long for Janos to learn just how tough it was. In *I Ain't Got Time to Bleed*, Ventura tells about a big mistake he made during the second day when he developed four or five blisters on each hand after running an obstacle course. His training instructor, Terry "Mother" Moy, called the broken blisters "flappers." Ventura recounts what happened:
>
> "All right. Which of you . . . has flappers?"
>
> Like an idiot, I raised my hand, "I do, Moy!"
>
> "Come on up here, boy!"
>
> I figured he was going to put Mercurochrome on them, so I stood up. "Hold your hands out." I put them out. "Are you right-handed or left-handed?" "Right-handed." I held it up. He grabbed every flap of skin and ripped them off, leaving my hand raw and throbbing. I had tears running down my face from the pain.
>
> Do you know why he asked me whether I was right-handed or left-handed? Because when he was done, he said, "Now, you do the other hand." So I had to stand in front of the class with Moy and pull my own flappers off. When I was done, he said, "You big dummy, now get back in line."

Did you grow up there?

Absolutely.

Were you a different person when you came out of [the SEALs]?

Completely.

Have you remained that person ever since?

Yes. Because no matter what I do now, that is the scale, that is the measuring stick. And no matter what adversities I face in life, I always go back to [SEALs] training and I say, This is nothing compared to that. It is like our slogan . . . "The Only Easy Day Was Yesterday." That says it all.[39]

A second legacy from his service as a SEAL was a more muscular physique, one that would help Janos make the transition to Jesse "The Body" Ventura a few years later. Ventura explains:

> During my last year, I had gotten into weight lifting. My intention was to play pro football when I got out, so the extra muscle would help give me an edge. The extra muscle [he now weighed 226 pounds] didn't get me into pro football. But it did help when I started on the wrestling circuit a few years later. So it is fairly easy for me to say where I stand now came directly from my time in the Teams. And that is a time that I will never forget. You can leave the Navy, but you never really leave the Teams.[40]

Chapter 3

Jesse "The Body" Ventura

IN THE NAVY, young Jim Janos had become "Janos the Dirty." Just a few years later he was reborn as Jesse Ventura, the ring alias he adopted as a professional wrestler. Ventura explains how and why he became Jesse Ventura:

> When you get into wrestling, you get to name yourself. And I always liked the name Jesse. And I was going to be a bleached blond from California because everyone hated bleached blondes from California. You know, throughout the rest of the country. And so I just started matching Jesse up with [names on] a map. And when I saw Jesse Ventura, the light went off.[41]

His journey from Navy SEAL to professional wrestler would be a bit like his search for a new name, when his eyes randomly darted across that California map to find Ventura, a Spanish word that means *luck* or *fortune*. After leaving the Navy, Janos would drift himself for several years, both geographically and personally, as he tried to figure out who he was and what he wanted to do.

Jim the Mongol

When his four-year tour of active duty ended in December 1973, Janos left the military, mostly because he did not like having to follow strict Navy rules and regulations. Janos still had to serve two years in the reserves, but he could fulfill that obligation anywhere. He decided to stay in California, where he had begun riding with a motorcycle gang called the Mongols:

My last six months in the Navy, I was riding with a local outlaw motorcycle club to keep the adrenaline moving. When I left the [base] area, I would put my colors [gang clothing] on and go off on my [Harley-Davidson motorcycle]. When I came back later, I would take off my colors and put on my Navy uniform. The attitude [of his superior officers] was that Janos would be getting out soon anyway, just leave him alone. As long as I was doing my job and kept my hair cut, things were fine with them.[42]

Janos had always loved the adrenaline rush he got from competitive sports and other physical challenges, and his work as a SEAL further addicted him to action and adventure; riding with a motorcycle gang was one way to continue living life on the edge. But even though he craved excitement, Janos was too honest to get involved in criminal activities. "I've never been arrested in my life. Never had cuffs put on me, never been charged with a crime, never spent one day in jail,"[43] he says. The bikers knew this and they would ask Janos to go sit with the bikes when they discussed any criminal activity. "Just because I wanted to have my fun," Ventura says, "didn't mean I couldn't keep my head screwed on right."[44]

Although he stayed with the Mongols for about six months after leaving the service, Janos held several jobs, including a brief stint as a bodyguard for the legendary rock 'n' roll group the Rolling Stones, one of his favorite bands. When Steve Nelson roomed with him after his Navy enlistment ended, Nelson discovered he still deserved the nickname "Janos the Dirty" because the floor of his apartment was strewn with motorcycle parts. But in early 1974, still uncertain what direction to take in life, Janos moved back to Minneapolis.

A College Student

In the spring of 1974 Janos enrolled in North Hennepin Community College, a two-year school in the suburb of Brooklyn Park, and that summer went out for football. Number 70 was an aggressive defensive lineman who liked to celebrate after making a tackle, taking off his helmet and strutting for the crowd. But the Navy veteran had trouble fitting in with his younger teammates, resented taking orders from his coach, and quit:

> I soured on football real fast. I was a twenty-two-year-old freshman, and after four years in the Navy, I'd played man's ultimate game, which is war. There is no way I could view football the way the coaches did—as a life-and-death struggle.[45]

Although Janos got good grades, school once again failed to capture his interest and he left after one year. But in March 1975, while he was still a student, Janos made his acting debut in a part that was perfect for someone heavily muscled from lifting weights—Hercules in the ancient Greek play *The Birds,* by Aristophanes. Janos liked the experience and took several classes in theater and acting, lessons that would help him later in his varied careers as a wrestler, actor, announcer, and politician.

Although the federal government was helping pay for his schooling because he was a veteran, Janos had to work. One of his jobs was as a bouncer in a bar called the Rusty Nail in Crystal, a Minneapolis suburb. It was there on a Thursday night in September 1974 that Janos met his future wife, Teresa Masters, an eighteen-year-old graduate of St. Louis Park High School, called Terry by her friends. Masters remembers being impressed the first time she saw Jim. "He was huge, with giant, broad shoulders, a gorgeous sport coat, wonderful slacks, and he had this white-blond hair and the most piercing blue eyes you could imagine," she says. "We locked eyes. I was awestruck."[46]

Janos was equally dazzled by the slim, beautiful young woman with long dark hair who, at five-feet-six-and-one-half inches, was nearly a foot shorter than he was. Masters didn't know it, but the bruising bouncer was training to become a professional wrestler.

Turning Pro

As boys, Jim and Jan Janos had listened to wrestling on the radio. Back home as adults, they began attending matches at the

A Brief History of Pro Wrestling

Professional wrestling has been popular in America for more than a century. In a story in the *Washington Post*, Jake Tapper tells how the sport developed:

> Pro wrestling has been a sport of cyclical popularity in the United States. At the turn of the century, Frank Gotch, the Babe Ruth of pro wrestling, was twice invited to Teddy Roosevelt's White House. There was even talk of his running for governor of Iowa—until he dropped dead in 1917 at the age of thirty-nine. The sport increased in popularity with the advent of television. "It was hot on TV in the late '40s and '50s since it was so easy to shoot," says Mike Chapman, executive director of the International Wrestling Institute and Museum in Newton, Iowa. But soon that popularity dissipated, and the sport retreated to a localized system of promotion. It was still huge in Minnesota, however, where the American Wrestling Association, run by Verne Gagne, was almighty. Gagne, a former University of Minnesota all-American and an alternate member of the 1948 Olympic team, had made a very successful jump to pro wrestling. From the '60s on, he based himself in Minneapolis, where he offered bulky guys who could wrestle a shot at a living and a modicum of fame, in the process building the AWA into one of the largest of the two dozen or so regional leagues operating around the country. For generations, the two dozen or so regional fiefdoms in pro wrestling had enjoyed a gentlemen's agreement in which cooperation was the norm. But with the growing markets of cable TV and pay-per-view, there was too much money pouring into the sport for those friendly relationships to survive.

Minnesota Armory, where Jim revived his childhood dream of becoming a wrestler:

> Out came Superstar Billy Graham. I had been pumping iron now for a year so I was starting to get buff and big, but this guy was beyond belief. He had twenty-two-and-a-half inch arms, he had bleached blond hair. He got into the ring and posed and my mind was set at that point. I wanted to do what the Superstar did. He was my hero.[47]

Janos went to Minneapolis's Seventh Street Gym, operated by Eddie Sharkey, who trained young wrestlers. Janos was already in great physical shape, heavily muscled at six-feet-four-inches and 260 pounds, and because he was a good athlete, it did not take him long to learn the basic moves. After training for only seven months, he turned pro in April 1975 when Bob Geigel, a promoter from Kansas City, Missouri, asked him to join the National Wrestling Alliance.

It was then that Jim Janos became Jesse Ventura. At first he was known as "Surfer" Jesse Ventura, but fans eventually began calling him "The Body" because of his impressive physique. Ventura became a wrestling star, but it was not easy.

Learning the Ropes

Professional wrestling is a hybrid of entertainment and athletics, not a real competition but more of an exaggerated morality play in which good and evil characters act out assigned parts. Ventura understood this. He had also decided to be a bad guy, a *heel* in ring parlance, like his idol, Billy Graham. Former wrestler Champ Thomas explains the two distinct roles wrestlers assume:

> The heels radiate hate and evil. The babyfaces [the good guys] project an all-American boy image. The heels rant and rave and shout like insane animals as they insist that they will demolish their opponents. The babyfaces insist that they'd rather stick to the rules but, if the bad guys get out of line, they [the babyfaces] will employ killer tactics to destroy them.[48]

Janos chose his ring name carefully as part of his calculated effort to develop a dramatic, villainous persona that would make fans notice him. "I knew that everybody hated beach bums," Ventura says. "They figured that beach bums spent their lives doing nothing but hanging out in the surf, getting tans, and chasing women. So I kept my bleached blond hair, wore outrageous sunglasses, earrings, and the big feather boas that later became my trademark."[49]

His fifty-two-inch chest, thirty-four-inch waist and nineteen-inch biceps also helped him become well known, the key to becoming a star. In his first match in Wichita, Kansas, he was disqualified for throwing babyface Omar Atlas over the ropes. Ventura had earned only a small sum, but he was on his way. He began wrestling for $35 to $65 a match in Missouri and Kansas while trying to build a reputation. After several months Ventura advanced to the Pacific Northwest circuit in Oregon, competing in such cities as Portland, Eugene, and Salem. He worked hard, driving 128,000 miles from fight to fight in less than two years, and he once wrestled sixty-three days in a row.

Attaining Stardom

Fans enjoyed his performances because of his outrageous personality, not his wrestling skills. As he became more popular, wrestling promoters in 1975 allowed him to win the Pacific Northwest heavyweight championship. To get the title he beat such opponents as Jimmy "Superfly" Snuka and Moondog Mayne in scripted matches that eventually transformed him from a heel into a babyface, a common practice when wrestlers become fan favorites. He won the title October 17, 1975, by defeating Snuka.

His big break came in 1979, when he was considered good enough to join the American Wrestling Association (AWA), the most prominent of the nation's more than two dozen regional circuits. The AWA was based in Minneapolis and run by Verne Gagne, a former collegiate and pro star. Wrestling throughout the Midwest, "The Body" was teamed with Adrian "Golden Boy" Adonis and on July 20, 1980, they won the AWA tag team championship. In tag team competition, pairs of wrestlers fight each other, but only one member of each team is allowed in the ring at the same time; partners trade places by tagging each other.

Ventura and Adonis were cast as heels and Ventura loved to inflame crowds with his antics. He would pose like a bodybuilder, sneer, yell at fans, and do anything he could to bolster his bad boy image:

> It was exciting. And for an ex-Navy SEAL, it was fun. It gets your adrenaline going. That's what it was like in the good old days of wrestling. Me and Adrian Adonis, the East-West connection [their nickname]—they got so mad at us in Sioux Falls, South Dakota, that the fans broke the dressing room door in half trying to get at us. The police were out there with nightsticks beating them off.[50]

Although a fine athlete and someone who could fight for real using his SEAL training, Ventura was a better talker and strutter than he was a wrestler. "His best move," says Dave Meltzer, editor of *Wrestling Observer Newsletter,* "was standing on the [ring] apron yelling at the fans while his tag team partner did all the work."[51] His signature wrestling hold was a simple one, "The Backbreaker," in which he would grab an opponent around the waist, hoist him across his shoulder, and then jump up and down until the wrestler gave up. Ventura developed a caustic rivalry with Hulk Hogan, who has ridiculed Ventura's wrestling prowess by saying, "Jesse's greatest move was to choke people, poke them in the eyes, and then run for his life."[52]

But in the crazy world of wrestling, it is not the best wrestlers who are stars but the most colorful personalities, the ones who excite the fans and draw them to arenas. Performing was something Ventura loved because of the feeling of power it gave him:

Jesse "The Body" Ventura pounds on the head of Hulk Hogan in one of their many featured wrestling matches.

I'll never forget [in 1981] the first time I sold out the St. Paul Civic Center and I walked in the ring. And I started my strut as I went in with my blond hair and I threw it back. And the crowd, nineteen-thousand of them, were chanting "Jesse Sucks" in unison. To have them in the palm of your hand and control them emotionally like that is a powerful feeling. It's the power of performing.[53]

By the early 1980s Ventura was earning $100,000 a year. He needed all the money he could make because he now had a wife, son, and daughter to support.

A Good Family Man

Ventura and Terry Masters were married July 18, 1975, in Timothy Evangelical Lutheran Church in St. Louis Park, less than a year after meeting at the Rusty Nail. He was twenty-four and she was nineteen and they went ahead with the ceremony despite the opposition of her parents. "[They thought] I was a bit eccentric and off the wall because I had bleached blond hair down to my shoulders, I chewed tobacco and I wasn't quite what they thought their daughter should marry,"[54] Ventura recalls. They were wrong; Ventura would be a good husband and father.

The couple had dated until Ventura began wrestling in Kansas City, but Ventura was so lonely after a couple of months that he asked Terry to visit him. She did, but was appalled at the shabby room he was renting in a cheap hotel for $23 a week. Ventura missed her even more after that and finally called to ask her to live with him. Masters said no and Ventura recalls what he did next:

> Being the typical noncommittal bachelor that I was, at first I just asked her to come down and live with me. She had a job [as a receptionist] and her own apartment; she was very self-sufficient, and she said, "I ain't leavin' up here unless I get a bigger commitment than 'Come on down and live with me.'" So, over the phone, I said, "Well, I guess I'll just have to say, 'Will you marry me?'" And she started crying and said yes.[55]

A Disastrous First Date

The first date Jesse Ventura and Teresa Masters went on was almost their last. Ventura was only a few years older than Terry, but he had experienced much more of the rawer side of life. While overseas, he had gone to bars and associated with prostitutes. Dating a young woman recently graduated from high school was entirely different. In a televised biography of Ventura on cable TV's A&E Channel, Terry talked about that first date:

> I bought all these new clothes and I was so excited. He told me he was going to take me to the Yacht Club. The Yacht Club turns out to be a hangout called the Schooner, it was a bar in south Minneapolis where all his buddies went. You could spit tobacco on the floor and there were brawls. The first night I was there the police went out and dragged some guy off his girlfriend he was beating the tar out of. I was just sitting there with my mouth open saying, "Who are these people?"

But Terry kept dating this seeming wild man because she recognized he had a kinder, gentler side. "When we were alone together," she said, "he was very quiet and very gallant and very peaceful within himself." And they were soon in love for good.

Ventura's wife, Terry, watches proudly as he is sworn in as governor of Minnesota. When the couple met, Ventura was a bouncer in a bar.

After the marriage Ventura began living a strange double life, one that would have stunned wrestling fans. As "The Body" he was a villainous, egotistical, raunchy extrovert. But when he climbed through the ropes and took off his pink tights, he became Jesse Ventura, loving husband. Even though he was on the road wrestling for weeks at a time, he did not succumb to the temptations that have snared so many other professional athletes: alcohol, drugs, and casual sex.

After his matches he would go back to his hotel, call Terry, and watch movies while he ate. "I kept my private life private," Ventura explains, "and that allowed me, for lack of a better word, to step out of character when I went back to my hotel room. I was not Jesse 'The Body' any more. I put so much into [that character] that when I got back to the hotel room it was a point of relief [to drop the persona]."[56]

Terry never worried about her husband misbehaving and Jesse says the separations never hurt their marriage. "Your time together is so precious," he says, "that you avoid fighting. Partly what made us strong is the fact that we would have such quality time together when I did come home."[57]

The quality time soon involved their children. Tyrel was born in 1979 and Jade in 1983. Small because he was a month premature, Tyrel—named by Ventura after a character in a Louis L'Amour Western novel—instantly captured the heart of the burly wrestler fans loved to hate. "I was the first to hold him in the world and he looked up at me and smiled," Ventura remembers. "And I'll never forget that. You've got him in the palm of your hand and he looks up at you and smiles."[58]

His daughter's birth, however, was an ordeal. When Terry went three weeks past her due date, labor had to be induced, and Jade began having epileptic seizures. "The very worst moment of my life," Ventura says, "came after my daughter, Jade, was born. The doctors immediately put her in intensive care because she was suffering from seizures. They told us she might never be able to lead a normal life. It was shattering and I tried to be strong."[59]

The seizures continued for six months, until doctors finally ended them with injections of a form of Vitamin B. When Jade

Governor Jesse Ventura smiles happily after his inauguration, along with his daughter, Jade, his wife, Terry, and his son, Tyrel.

was nine months old, however, she had a severe reaction to a routine vaccination against childhood diseases, and the episode caused permanent neurological damage. But with the help of a loving mother and father, and a protective big brother, Jade has led a normal life despite such early developmental problems as poor coordination, motor skills, and reflexes. Jade did not walk until age two and attended special-education classes in school, but as a teenager she would win trophies for riding horses and learn to play the piano and flute. "Thankfully, the doctors were wrong," Ventura says about predictions Jade would never be able to lead a normal life. "She is my inspiration—a reminder of what faith and determination can accomplish."[60]

The WWF Emerges

Having children made it more important for Ventura to become a star, so he could give them a comfortable lifestyle. Although he was earning about $100,000 a year in the AWA, Ventura in

1984 jumped for good to the fledgling World Wrestling Federation (WWF) run by Vince McMahon Jr. Ventura had wrestled in the WWF in 1981 and 1982 before returning to the AWA, where he eventually clashed with Gagne.

Two years earlier, McMahon had bought his father's wrestling business, the New York–based Capitol Wrestling Corporation, and made a bold decision: he would no longer honor the traditional boundaries of other wrestling circuits. McMahon began televising WWF bouts to other regions of the country, and after the TV shows made his stars well known, he would stage live fights in those regions. McMahon used television to make his federation the most successful in wrestling history and to propel the sport to new heights of popularity.

McMahon had begun raiding the AWA talent pool and in 1984 sought Ventura, who wasn't sure what to do; he had a family to care

Vince McMahon, the promoter who created the World Wrestling Federation and helped make Jesse "The Body" Ventura a national celebrity.

for and moving to the WWF was a decision that could turn out badly. Ventura biographer Tapper explains the risks:

> Jesse and Terry went out to talk about the [move]. It was risky, and he'd be burning his bridges with Gagne, no question. Maybe even burning the bridges with the old guard, because they hated Vince Jr. and what he was doing. There was a chance that, if Vince Jr. failed, Jesse might never wrestle again. Nonetheless, they decided to go for it.[61]

A Bigger Star than Ever

Agonizing as it had been to make, the decision turned out well as the WWF began to attract larger audiences than wrestling ever had before. Along with former AWA star Hulk Hogan, Ventura was one of the WWF's top drawing cards, and in 1984 he and Adonis were profiled in *People* magazine. Ventura's fame had begun to spread outside the wrestling world, he was earning more money, and he was going to get a shot at taking the WWF title away from Hogan. Life was good for the former Navy SEAL and his family.

Chapter 4

Jesse "The Mouth" Ventura

I<small>N</small> 1984 J<small>ESSE</small> "The Body" Ventura was at the height of his fame and glory, touring thirty cities in a series of bouts against reigning champion Hulk Hogan that were scheduled to culminate in a WWF title match in Los Angeles. But the biggest fight of Ventura's career never occurred. Instead, Ventura found himself fighting for his life in Sharp Cabrillo Hospital in San Diego after a blood clot broke loose from a vein in his leg and lodged in his lung. It was one of the worst things that ever happened to him:

> I think the lowest part of my life was when I was hit with pulmonary emboli the night I was due to wrestle Hulk Hogan for the world title in L.A. and it was sold out. I was going around the circuit with him everywhere in the nation and I bet it cost me well over a million [dollars]. But, you know, a lot of good came out of that bad incident. Because it was through that low point that I became an announcer and it led me into a new field that later on, when I got too old to wrestle, I could continue on with. But that was the lowest point also because I was critical for six days, and my wife had to fly to San Diego to be at my bedside.[62]

The hulking physique that had seen him safely through the rigors of life as a Navy SEAL and made him rich and famous as a wrestler had betrayed him. He would now have to rely more than ever on the one part of his body he could still count on—his mouth, which would enable him to work as an announcer of wrestling and football, an actor in television and films, and a radio talk show host.

Ring Announcer

Ventura's illness convinced him that he had to give up wrestling. Although wrestling matches are staged, the falls and physical blows combatants suffer can and do injure them. Ventura had always felt his share of aches and pains after bouts and the nagging injuries had become more persistent as he got older. Now, with the threat of more life-threatening blood clots if his body kept absorbing such terrific daily punishment, Ventura knew he had to quit. At age thirty-three, "The Body" had to find a new way to support a wife, a five-year-old son, and a one-year-old daughter who had severe medical problems. "It's a traumatic moment for any professional athlete to face," Ventura says. "What do you do when it's over? What happens when your body can't perform any more? Where do you go from here?"[63]

But in early 1985, while still recovering from the blood clot, Ventura got a call from WWF owner McMahon that opened a door to a new life. McMahon wanted the popular wrestler to become the first bad guy announcer, a heel with a microphone who could root for the bad guys and spice up telecasts with funny, caustic, off-the-wall remarks. It was a job perfectly suited for Ventura, who had become a star more for his bombastic personality than his limited wrestling ability.

His arch rival, Hogan, had once commented on Ventura's lack of ring technique: "Jesse's best move was to cheat and run."[64] But in wrestling, bad guys are supposed to cheat. When Ventura became an announcer he articulated the strategy that had served him well: "Win if you can, lose if you must, but always cheat."[65] Ventura was only kidding about cheating, but that and other colorful, inflammatory comments, like the time he claimed wrestling star Ultimate Warrior had a million-dollar body and a ten-cent brain, made him a hit. "Right out of the gate, he was very good," remembers "Mean Gene" Okerlund, the veteran ring announcer Ventura often worked with. "If someone else was talking, Jesse was listening and thinking. He developed a very quick wit."[66]

When an injury made "The Body" give up his ring appearances, he switched to commenting on matches, which earned him a new nickname —Jesse "The Mouth" Ventura.

But Jesse "The Mouth," as Ventura now became known, was sometimes criticized for remarks that could be considered to be in poor taste or, even worse, racial slurs. He called African American wrestler Koko B. Ware "Buckwheat," the name of a stereotypical African American character in the old Our Gang comedies. He characterized the moves of the Junk Yard Dog, another African American, as "a lot of shuckin' and jivin'." Ventura defended himself by saying that Ware had given him permission to use the nickname "Buckwheat" and claimed his comments were only part of the fake framework of professional wrestling:

When I participated in [wrestling], it was built on stereotypes. Every Japanese wrestler threw salt and was sneaky, every German wrestler was a Nazi, every Russian a communist. How could anyone possibly look at wrestling and say, "This is what he believes in?" It's entertainment. My job was to irritate people. Another of my infamous wrestling quotes was, "Win if you can, lose if you must, but always cheat." And some people drum that up today like it's some policy. All of a sudden wrestling's real to them? C'mon.[67]

Ventura, who received only about $800 for his first announcing jobs, eventually earned as much as $7,500 for *Saturday Night Main Events* and $20,000 for such widely publicized extravaganzas as *WrestleMania IV*. In 1988 he was also a special referee for the WWF's first *SummerSlam* pay-per-view event. His new celebrity and obvious dexterity delivering words helped pave the way for another new career—as an actor.

Jesse the Actor

In 1985, when Ventura was cast as a villain on the television show *Hunter*, he found that acting came naturally. After all, Jim Janos had been playing the part of the wild-eyed Jesse "The Body" Ventura for years while remaining, in his private life, much the same person he had been while growing up in Minnesota. Ventura would later have small parts in several television shows, including a 1996 episode of *The X-Files*, a failed TV pilot called *Tag Team* with fellow wrestler "Rowdy" Roddy Piper, and starring roles in some commercials. But his main acting career has been on the big screen.

With the help of agent Barry Bloom, Ventura won an audition for the film *Predator* with Arnold Schwarzenegger, the Austrian bodybuilder who had become an action star. *Predator* became a hit, catapulting Ventura to new heights of fame as he was seen by tens of millions of moviegoers around the world. "It was by far the best film of my career," Ventura says. "People say I stole the film from Arnold. Fox [studio] even made a T-shirt with my famous line, 'I ain't got time to bleed.' Taking that role was one of the best decisions in my life."[68]

Jesse Ventura: Movie Star

By the time Jesse Ventura started acting, he had been a celebrity for more than a decade. But in an interview with Britt Robson in *City Pages*, a Minneapolis newspaper, Ventura acknowledged that making movies changed the way he was treated:

> [I remember] the premiere of *Predator* and becoming a real full-fledged movie star and going on an 18-day press junket with Arnold Schwarzenegger. That was a trip into the twilight zone. From South Minneapolis to riding on a private jet that holds like 14 people, and there are only two or three people on it beside the pilots, and to be staying in hotels where the cheapest room was $800 a night. I left to do that press junket with $234 in my pocket and my credit cards, and I returned never having used my credit cards once and with $234 still in my wallet. And being treated like—well, like a movie star. Where everything is paid for you and you eat in the finest restaurants in the land and order room service. At the time I was chewing tobacco, and every city you would land in there was someone to cater to you. I flew to Chicago, and I was out of chewing tobacco at the time and I said to this guy, "By the way, I need a can of Copenhagen." The guy ran off immediately and came back within 45 minutes with a shopping bag full, and he said, "Is that enough?" I thought, God Almighty, I could service Major League Baseball with what you've got for me. So I said, "Yeah, it's enough."

Jesse Ventura and Bill Duke in the hit movie Predator. *In his role as Sergeant Blain, Ventura delivered the famous line, "I ain't got time to bleed."*

Ventura Plays a Trick on Arnold Schwarzenegger

Ventura claims that one of the best things that happened to him when he started making films was to meet Arnold Schwarzenegger, who became a close friend. The two huge men, one a former wrestler and the other a famous bodybuilder, bonded while filming *Predator*. In *I Ain't Got Time to Bleed*, Ventura recounts a practical joke he played on his new friend:

> Arnold is terrific. He's a generous guy. When he got down there, he had all of his gym equipment put into a room, and he gave a key to me and anyone else who wanted one and said, "Work out whenever you want to." We got up in the mornings and worked out from five to six, because if we didn't Arnold would be on our cases all day.... So I started getting up at about quarter to five and getting into the gym before Arnold and his friend Sven (his bodyguard and double) came in. I would grab the mineral water and soak myself with it, so I would look like I was drenched with sweat. I would only be doing my first set when Sven and Arnold walked in, but Arnold didn't know that! He'd walk in and say, "Sven! Look at this! Who knows how long Jesse's been training! We must get up earlier. We can't let Jesse outtrain me!" So it ended up that we were both getting up earlier and earlier, until we were getting up at four in the morning!

Filming began April 8, 1986, and for $5,000 a week Ventura tramped around wild jungle areas in Jalisco, Palenque, and Puerto Vallarta in Mexico while playing the part of Sergeant Blain, a wise-cracking, tobacco-chewing former commando. The part was tailor-made for Ventura, who at the time was still chewing tobacco, a vice he had picked up as a SEAL. Schwarzenegger, however, got his co-star and new friend to exchange that bad habit for cigars, which Schwarzenegger puffed on in real life as well as in his part as the leader of the commando unit.

In *Predator*, Schwarzenegger's commandos head into the jungle of a nameless South American country to rescue two officials taken prisoner by guerrilla rebels. An alien monster with chameleon-like camouflage skills starts hunting and killing the commandos. Blain is the second one to be slaughtered, but not before uttering his famous, macho line about having no time to bleed.

Schwarzenegger liked Ventura so much that he cast him in another science fiction film, *The Running Man*, that appeared in 1987. Like *Predator*, the movie featured heavy doses of fighting, blood, and gore; its plot revolved around a savage television game show of the future. *Chicago Sun-Times* film critic Roger Ebert gave the film this review:

> *The Running Man* is an arcade game for the big screen, a contest in which the player is Arnold Schwarzenegger and the game keeps throwing big bruisers at him. To cast this movie, they called up the reserves of Hollywood heavies. There are villains named Fireball, Captain Freedom [Ventura's character], Dynamo, Buzzsaw and Subzero, all thrown at Arnold like new chapters in a superhero comic book, and with true comic justice, each villain dies by his own weapon. The cast reads like a roll call of action heroes and pro wrestlers: Jim Brown, Jesse Ventura, Erland Van Lidth, Professor Toru.[69]

Jesse Ventura, as he appeared in The Running Man, *an action film starring his friend, Arnold Schwarzenegger. Neither Ventura's performance nor the movie were very good and he never became a successful actor.*

Although Ventura's salary had quadrupled to $20,000 a week, his part as Captain Freedom was not very big and the movie was not very good, comments that could also be applied in general to his film career. In the next few years Ventura played several other small parts, including a sports commentator in *No Holds Barred* starring Hulk Hogan, and an asylum guard in *Batman & Robin*. His only starring role was in *Abraxas, Guardian of the Universe*, a low-budget film in 1991 that cast him in the role of Earth's savior. The following review is from the Amazing World of Cult Movies Internet site:

> Minnesota governor Jesse Ventura stars in this pathetic attempt to cash in on *T2: Judgment Day* [a hit film starring Schwarzenegger]. Ventura's a bounty-hunter from outer space who falls in love with a human woman (Marjorie Bransfield) who was impregnated five years before when touched by a nasty alien (Sven-Ole Thorsen). Her kid (Frances Mitchell) is mute and has superhuman powers. Jim Belushi is around in his usual guise as a school principal, and Marilyn Lightstone co-stars with Jerry Levitan and director Damian Lee, who also made *Food of the Gods 2* and *Ski School*. Ventura's character, Abraxas, is 11,856 years old.[70]

The movie received poor reviews and Ventura began to have trouble getting film work. However, his concern for his family also hurt his movie career when he refused to move to California, believing that Tyrel and Jade were better off growing up in Minnesota. "I might have gone a lot further in Hollywood if I had been willing to move there," Ventura says. "I know it hurt my film career, but so be it. My kids come first."[71]

Radio Work

When good acting jobs failed to materialize, Ventura started using his mouth in a new medium. His voice is distinctive, deep, and slightly gravelly, perfect for capturing the attention of listeners. In 1989 the high school and Navy football star who at one time dreamed of playing in the National Football League began working as a color commentator for Tampa Bay

> ### Ventura's Starring Role
> Jesse Ventura received $250,000 for starring in *Abraxas, Guardian of the Universe*. Filming began in November 1989 in a small community northeast of Toronto, Canada, and Ventura earned every penny, often under miserable circumstances because the low-budget movie was shot outdoors in the dead of winter. Biographer Jake Tapper recounts the ordeal Ventura had to go through to film scenes involving a lake:
>> For some of the scenes, Jesse had to stand dressed in skimpy clothing, outdoors, and in water. "The water was cold enough to induce hypothermia," [director Damian] Lee says. "We had to cut holes in the ice for him. There was a physical threat of a very real nature." It's impossible to know what got Jesse to actually take the plunge—his machismo, the money, the potential of fame for his first starring role, or just the fact that he had agreed to do so—but he did.
>> "Damian," Jesse said as he marched toward the lake, "I'm not going in this water."
>> "Jess, I think that's a good idea," Lee replied.
>> Jesse kept walking. "I'm not going in," he'd repeat.
>> "Good idea, Jess," returned Lee. "It's too cold today."
>> Then he'd march right into the water and Lee would yell "Action!"

Buccaneers games. He was hired as a celebrity to liven up broadcasts for a losing team that had trouble attracting fans.

Gene Deckerhoff called the plays and Al Keck analyzed the action, with Ventura providing some general, colorful comments. "I like the way that guy's hittin'—that's real football,"[72] Ventura would growl after a particularly brutal tackle. Ventura's remarks were simple, to the point, and, as always, a reflection of his personality. He worked games for the 1989–90 and 1990–91 seasons before the Florida radio station decided to scrap the three-man format and did not renew the announcers' contracts.

But Ventura had done so well that he was hired the next season by Minneapolis station KFAN-FM to do Minnesota Vikings games. Once again the big wrestler was squeezed into a booth with two others, play-by-play announcer Dan Rowe and analyst Dave Huffman, a former Viking lineman. "He offered kind of a glorified fan's appraisal of the game as it went along," Rowe recalls. "His value to the whole picture was that he didn't mince any words."[73]

A veteran radio talk show host, Governor Jesse Ventura broadcasts live from the Minnesota State Fair in August 1999. The governor went on the air weekly to talk to his constituents.

The experiment did not work very well and Ventura was released after one season. However, "The Mouth" was a hit with Viking players, who could relate to him because of his size, athletic background, and fondness for weight lifting. The players even enjoyed making jokes at his expense, something normal sized people usually are afraid to do. Ventura at the time had shaved his head except for a small tail that hung low from the back of his skull; the players kidded him about it, claiming he looked like a Hare Krishna, a member of a Hindu religious group.

When Ventura's football work proved he could handle radio broadcasting, KSTP-FM in Minneapolis decided to give him his own talk show. *The Jesse Ventura Show* went on the air in January 1993, with the former wrestler dispensing his views on a variety of subjects from 5:30 A.M. until 9 A.M. each weekday. Politics became one of his favorite topics, including his obsession with the mystery surrounding the 1963 assassination of President John Kennedy. Ventura was as caustic in his attacks on elected officials as he had been about wrestlers, but one comment would cost him his job.

On May 5, 1995, he labeled Minnesota state representative Myron Orfield a communist, stirring up controversy over his lack of restraint. Ventura later amended the charge to socialist but continued attacking the liberal legislator and refused to issue a genuine apology. KSTP, fearful that Ventura would say something even more controversial, fired him, a situation that was tough for Ventura to handle. "I had never been fired before, and they fired me six months into a two-year contract," he recalls. "I went through a period of about a year where I didn't have a job. And it made me vulnerable because when you're at that age, changing careers and stuff becomes [frightening]."[74]

When the station tried to renege on his contract, Ventura threatened legal action, which forced the station to give him a financial settlement. Ventura was unemployed for almost a year except for some work in Hollywood, but in 1997 KFAN put him on the air again in *Pure Ventura:*

> My radio show, although it was basically sports oriented, took on a sharp political edge. In between discussing games, I railed at government overspending. I ragged on bloated bureaucracy, and I roasted corrupt government officials. The KFAN people liked to send me out to do shows outside the studio, because I did really well with a live audience. Every Friday they'd send me out to a family restaurant, and I'd do "Paycheck Friday." I'd say, "Let's see who the government took the most from this week," and I'd have people bring up their pay stubs.[75]

Wrestling the WWF

Paychecks and making money are always on Ventura's mind. Over the years he has learned to make the most of his celebrity to provide for his family, and on March 31, 1992, he even copyrighted the name Jesse "The Body" Ventura with the U.S. Patent and Trademark Office. His legal name, however, was still James George Janos, even though most people knew him only as Jesse Ventura.

A son of working-class parents who had to work hard for everything they had, Ventura was always willing to fight for every penny he thought he had coming. That included challenging the WWF in a lawsuit in 1991 after he learned it was making money from his name and likeness through the sales of videotapes of wrestling events and a wide variety of related merchandise. Biographer Jake Tapper details the money involved:

> The WWF's parent company, Titan, and its business partners had sold more than $25 million in videotapes on which Jesse appeared, $2 million of Jesse dolls, $144,000 worth of 1987 and 1988 calendars featuring Jesse's likenesses as both a WWF announcer and in *Predator,* $730,000 worth of computer games, $2.4 million of trading cards and [untold amounts] in T-shirts and other souvenirs.[76]

It took several years for the lawsuit to wend its way through the court system, but on July 21, 1994, the WWF was ordered to pay Ventura $809,958.66 in compensation, $85,568.20 in interest, and $66.57 per day from that date until it paid Ventura what it owed him. The settlement was Ventura's biggest payday ever for winning a fight, even if the battle had been waged in a courtroom instead of the ring.

By taking on the WWF, Ventura had shown a willingness to stand up for what he believed in, even if it meant risking his reputation and livelihood by taking on the organization that dominated professional wrestling. It was that same motivating spirit of fighting for what he thought was right that led him in 1990 to run for mayor of Brooklyn Park.

Chapter 5

Jesse "The Mayor" Ventura

ALTHOUGH MOST PEOPLE would never have expected it of a wrestler who became famous wearing pink tights and feather boas, Jesse Ventura had always been keenly interested in politics. It was a lifelong passion that was ignited by his parents:

> I've got strong political opinions, and they took root early. Both of my folks could be very stubborn and bullheaded, but my dad was politically so. My first introduction to politics came early in life, over family dinner. We watched the news on TV while we ate, and he argued back to it whenever he heard something he didn't like. He ranted and raved and carried on to the point where my mom was ready to toss him down to the basement.[77]

In 1983 Ventura and his family moved to Brooklyn Park, a suburb ten miles northwest of the Twin Cities on the west bank of the Mississippi River. When explosive growth boosted its population from only sixteen thousand in 1972 to nearly sixty thousand in 1990, making it Minnesota's sixth largest city, Ventura began to be concerned about expansion problems, including rising taxes and damage to natural areas.

The issue that ignited his political career was a plan for a new subdivision near his home. Ventura was upset for two reasons: first, the plan called for adding curbs, gutters, and storm sewers to the area, improvements he did not feel necessary and which would mean a special assessment on his house; and second, the developers wanted to channel storm runoff into a local wetland, which could harm it. Ventura and his neighbors opposed the plan, but the city council voted 7–0 against their request to halt the subdivision. What upset Ventura the most was the lack of respect shown to opponents by Mayor Jim Krautkremer and six council members, who ignored a petition signed by more than 450 residents.

Ventura continued attending council sessions, helped a friend, Joe Enge, win a council seat, and spoke out at a meeting on what was wrong with Brooklyn Park. Terry Ventura says the arrogant way elected officials received her husband's comments infuriated him. "They were so rude," she says, "and Jesse just finally said,

Governor Jesse Ventura makes a point during a news conference on February 22, 1999, at the National Press Club in Washington, D.C.

'Look, you're going to make me run for mayor.' They laughed at him and said, 'You can't win.'"[78]

But *can't* is a word Ventura hates to hear. The sarcastic comment not only made him angry, it made him a candidate for mayor.

Winning an Election

Although Ventura had been too busy to engage in political or social causes, he was always interested in such issues. In the late 1970s he supported a movement to end the draft because he believed forced military service was wrong, even though he had fought in Vietnam, and in the 1980s he persuaded Terry to go with him to a rally in support of the Equal Rights Amendment, a proposed constitutional amendment guaranteeing women the same rights as men. In 1986 Ventura even tried to start a union to bolster the rights of wrestlers, a bold move in a profession controlled by promoters. Other wrestlers were afraid to join, but the effort was an indication "The Body" was willing to fight for what he believed was right.

Ventura decided it was necessary to replace Krautkremer, mayor since 1972, because he had lost touch with his constituents. As in wrestling, Ventura saw the fight as one between good and evil, only now he was the babyface. "I always believed that if you're gonna kill the snake, cut off the head,"[79] Ventura says. His fame brought a new level of excitement to the mayoral race and he attracted volunteers who had never been active in politics before, including Terry. "I threw myself into that race," she says. "I went door to door."[80] Only 2,632 voters had turned out in the 1986 election, but in 1990 an astounding 20,118 residents flocked to the polls.

Ventura energized a bored electorate to score a stunning landslide victory, beating the long-time incumbent with 65 percent of the vote. "My mom and dad were there that night to see my victory. They were very proud,"[81] he says.

The Mayor Wore Jeans

No city, especially not one like this small Midwestern community, ever had a mayor like Ventura. The city's new chief executive wore T-shirts and jeans to council meetings and wrapped a bandanna pirate-style around his head, which he had shaved, except for a small tail of hair at the nape of his neck. Ventura also acted unconventionally, suggesting in the first city council session that he wanted to scrap the traditional Roberts Rules of Order for conducting meetings because they were too confusing.

That was the first of many battles Ventura would lose, almost always by a 5-2 margin as he and Enge were outvoted on nearly every issue. In 1992 a second supporter, Grace Arbogast, was elected, but Ventura still kept losing 4-3. The mayor didn't care because he had won approval to televise meetings. "That way, everyone watching at home on cable TV saw our ideas were being voted down," Ventura says. "If people agreed with our ideas, well, then, it caused a lot of outrage among the citizens."[82]

The majority opposing him made it difficult for Ventura to accomplish what he wanted. One of his goals was reducing taxes, yet they rose every year he was in office. "The mayor,"

Why Jesse Ventura Ran for Mayor

In *The Wit and Wisdom of Jesse "The Body...The Mind" Ventura*, a collection of quotations on various subjects compiled by Jessica Allen, Ventura explains why he decided to run for mayor of Brooklyn Park:

> I sent my kids to public school and paid taxes. We had a little wetland in the neighborhood and we lived in an old part of Brooklyn Park where we all had ditches. Houses had been there for fifty, sixty years, and the city wanted to come in and give us curbs and gutters, storm drainage—all that stuff—but we as a neighborhood felt that money could be spent in a better way. Why spend money if no one's complaining and no one has a problem? To do it they had to pump storm sewer water to a little wetland and hurt it. [Ventura got together with 450 people to fight the development, but their measure opposing it was voted down 7-0.] Now I might have accepted four to three, but seven to zero is a slam dunk. I got a little upset over that. I started getting more involved in local Brooklyn Park politics. Then, when I got involved with another unrelated issue, the twenty-year incumbent mayor angered me, and just off the cuff I said, "You're going to make me run, aren't you?" The council laughed and said, "You could never win." Well, I ran and I won all twenty-one precincts, beat the mayor 65 percent to 35 percent, and he had the backing of both the Democrats and the Republicans in a nonpartisan election.

Ventura explains, "doesn't have very much power. I was only one vote out of seven on the city council, and it was always a five-two vote [on] taxes."[83] Terry claims the old guard council members not only worked to defeat her husband, but to make him an object of ridicule. "From the second he sat down and rapped the gavel," she says, "they were out to humiliate him publicly. [The term] was the most grueling four years I've ever spent."[84]

Ventura did have a few successes. In 1991 he went to Washington, D.C., and successfully lobbied for $36 million in federal funds for a highway spur through Brooklyn Park. He claims that one of his greatest accomplishments was to reduce crime through increased police patrols. He tells why more patrols were needed:

> Police are reactive, they're not proactive. Come up to any thirty-year veteran on the force and say, "How many crimes have you stopped in progress?" And he'll tell you honestly, "Maybe one or two." When you ask him, "Well, what allowed you to do that?" he's gonna tell you: "Luck. There was no rhyme nor reason to it. I happened to turn left and saw a guy dashing out of a house with a TV set." So if you're going to take a proactive stance to stop crime, you must have neighborhood involvement, your business community must become involved, and then the government must be there in a support fashion.[85]

But Don Davis, Brooklyn Park police chief from 1978 to 1993, says crime rates had begun to fall before Ventura took office due to community-oriented policing techniques Davis started in 1988. However, Davis praises Ventura for supporting police efforts, especially programs for young people.

Ventura declined to run for a second four-year term, claiming he had accomplished his mission. "I rode into town, I ran the bad guys out of town, and now it's time for me to ride into the sunset,"[86] he said dramatically. However, his critics have a different view of his tenure.

A Sometime Mayor?

Rick Engh, a council member for fourteen years, acted as mayor pro-tem when Ventura was away. And Ventura was absent a lot, missing almost 20 percent of council meetings while making movies, announcing wrestling matches, or working on other projects. Engh, who in 1992 was defeated for reelection by Arbogast, contends:

> I probably served more as mayor than he did. He was always away making movies and everything. He would sit there at meetings, chewing snuff and spitting in a cup. I thought that was rude and disrespectful to the audience.[87]

Engh also criticized the mayor's conduct, including chewing snuff at the same meeting Ventura was trying to pass a measure to ban tobacco ads and remove tobacco products from view in the city's retail food outlets. The measure eventually died.

Some people were also put off by Ventura's confrontational, intimidating personal style. In March 1993 council member Robert Stromberg angered Ventura by making a motion to appoint a new member to the police commission while the mayor was absent. Ventura verbally attacked him in the next meeting for trying to act behind his back, touching off the following exchange:

> Stromberg: I am not into intimidation or standing nose to nose and trying to punch it out with somebody. . . .
>
> Ventura: Neither am I.
>
> Stromberg: But that's exactly what you're doing right now. It's about the silliest thing I've ever seen.
>
> Ventura: But it's entertaining the folks back home.
>
> Stromberg: We're not here for entertainment.
>
> Ventura: I am.[88]

In the last six months of his term, Ventura created a final controversy when he bought a home in nearby Maple Grove. Ventura purchased the $500,000, thirty-two acre ranch and large house because his ill mother was now living with the family and they needed

Jesse "The Intimidator" Ventura?

During his reign as mayor, Jesse Ventura was accused of trying to intimidate political opponents, from council members to the news media. The following incident involving the editor of the *Sun Post*, Brooklyn Park's newspaper, is from a story by Kermit Pattison in *George* magazine:

> Harvey Rockwood is a small-town newspaperman who long ago grew accustomed to verbal assaults from angry readers. But one particular confrontation in 1993 stands out in his memory: the time a 250-pound former Navy SEAL, professional wrestler, and actor named Jesse "The Body" Ventura came after him. Ventura was then the mayor of Brooklyn Park, Minnesota. He was furious about an editorial that had appeared in that week's paper, which suggested that Ventura, who had transformed once staid City Council meetings into rowdy, partisan affairs, behaved more like an entertainer than a civic leader. Rockwood recalls that the mayor stormed up to him and growled, "Your newspaper said I was shit." Ventura pointed his index finger in Rockwood's face. "I don't think of myself as a wimp," the editor says. "But it was a fight-or-flight situation. I definitely chose flight." Six years later, Ventura puts that confrontation in another light. He says it was just part of his challenge to the city's good-old-boy network, and his face scrunches in annoyance upon hearing the newspaperman's account. "I never hit anyone," he insists. "I never threatened to hit anybody. I just can be pretty persuasive when I need to be."

Jesse Ventura has been accused of using his strong-willed personality and aggressive body language to intimidate political foes. His forceful gesture and stern look here came during his speech after he was sworn in as governor.

more room. To maintain his residency, he slept several nights a week in the Brooklyn Park house—sparsely furnished with two television sets, workout equipment, a radio, and a bed.

Even though Ventura had already announced he would not run for reelection, Stromberg and other detractors tried to oust him from office, claiming he no longer lived in the city. An administrative law judge, however, ruled Ventura was still a resident and could finish his term.

Ventura's Ventures

Another reason Ventura did not seek reelection was that KSTP had told him it would probably cancel his radio show if he ran because of federal rules mandating equal time for political candidates; the station would have had to give his opponent air time equal to the hours Ventura was on the air. And Ventura did not want to give up his show for a part-time job that paid $10,000 a year.

While he was mayor, Ventura acted in movies and announced matches for World Championship Wrestling (WCW), a circuit founded by news media mogul Ted Turner. Ventura had departed the WWF in 1991 after filing his lawsuit seeking video royalties. When Ventura debuted in February 1992 by announcing the *SuperBrawl II* pay-per-view show, the WCW trumpeted his return with the phrase "The Body Is Back."

This time, however, Ventura failed to appeal to the public, began fighting with his bosses over how to do his job, and in 1994 was released. Ventura claims he was forced out when his old enemy, Hulk Hogan, joined the WCW as its top attraction. But Dave Meltzer of *Wrestling Observer Newsletter* believes Ventura and some other announcers simply lost touch with the changing world of wrestling, which had new stars, new plot lines, and a new, hipper style. "What the [older] announcers knew just wasn't relevant anymore. And at the end, Jesse just lost a lot of interest,"[89] Meltzer says.

The Reform Party

As his movie and announcing jobs dried up, Ventura spent more time in Minneapolis and became increasingly involved in politics. Ventura used his radio show in 1994 to attack his old political foe, Stromberg, and help Arbogast beat Stromberg in the mayoral primary. He hosted U.S. Senate candidate Dean Barkley on his show in 1994 and two years later, when Barkley ran again, the Reform Party candidate named Ventura his honorary campaign chairman.

Barkley was running as a candidate for the Minnesota branch of the independent party that Texas millionaire Ross Perot started in 1992 when he ran for president. Ventura became interested in the Reform Party because it mirrored his stands on such issues as the need to pass stricter campaign finance laws and to set limits on the number of years officials can stay in office.

Like most third-party candidates, Barkley had trouble gaining name recognition because of a lack of funds for television and newspaper ads. When Ventura drew bigger cheers than he did during a Fourth of July campaign appearance, Barkley realized the former wrestler would be a stronger candidate. "I said, 'Jesse, the wrong person's running. This should be you.' That's when the lightbulb went on in my head that we had someone here who had the unique ability to connect to people,"[90] Barkley says.

Barkley lost but never forgot the crowd response to Ventura. For the next two years he tried to persuade Ventura to run in 1998 to replace popular two-term Governor Arne Carlson. Ventura was reluctant, but the issue that finally got him to run was a huge budget surplus Minnesota had built up in the economic boom of the late 1990s. Ventura started demanding on his talk show that the state return more than $1 billion to taxpayers. Like his father before him, Ventura had a basic distrust of politicians. His fear that elected officials would not return the surplus pushed him into the race:

> I believe in fate. I believe things happen for a reason. Things just fell into place. I started talking about that first budget surplus on talk radio and how it should have been given back, and callers were saying, "Well, why don't you run for governor?" and the whole thing escalated from there. It escalated to the point where I had to run, because if I hadn't, I'd have lost my credibility. I just got inspired to do it then. And then I got really inspired when everyone told me I couldn't win. I wish I had a dollar for every time I heard that.[91]

Jesse "The Coach" Ventura

Jesse Ventura, assistant coach, delivers some sideline advice to a Champlin Park High School player during a game November 16, 1998.

Newspaper, television, and magazine reporters lavished hundreds of column inches and hours of videotape on Jesse Ventura during the campaign. Reporters loved Ventura because he was more entertaining than other candidates. Almost every media outlet covered his part-time job coaching football at Champlin Park High School. This excerpt is from an article by Doug Grow of the Minneapolis *Star Tribune*:

> The candidate/coach pulled into the stadium parking lot about 6 P.M., driving a Porsche with a Navy SEALS slogan around the license plate. "Mess with the best," it says above the plate. "Die like the rest," it says below. As soon as Ventura arrived, Tim Hermann, Champlin Park's head coach, turned his team over to [Ventura]. The players stormed at Ventura, and together players and the volunteer coach stomped and chanted about what it takes to be No. 1.
>
> "What is pain?" Ventura yelled.
>
> "Pain is weakness leaving the body," the players, in unison, roared back.
>
> "Pain is good," Ventura yelled.
>
> "Extreme pain is extremely good," the players roared back.
>
> Then, players and Ventura did exercises, yelling out counts in unison and growling a lot between exercises.
>
> Thought: Minnesotans might become more fit under a Ventura administration. More vocal, too. Considerable commitment to state causes would be expected.

On January 26, 1998, Ventura announced his candidacy at the state capitol. He promised he would veto any tax increase, return the budget surplus to state residents, and not accept special interest money or any donation larger than $50.

The Campaign

The Democratic Party, officially known as the Democratic-Farmer-Labor Party in Minnesota, had nominated Hubert "Skip" Humphrey III—the state attorney general for fourteen years and son of Hubert Humphrey, the former governor, U.S. senator, and vice president who is Minnesota's most famous politician. The Republican candidate was St. Paul mayor Norm Coleman.

Running on the Reform Party ticket, Ventura faced huge odds in defeating the two major party candidates. His two biggest obstacles were a lack of campaign funds—he spent only $600,000, compared with the combined $13 million spent by his two opponents—and the fact that most people traditionally vote either Democratic or Republican. His two biggest advantages were his name recognition and the fact that he was not a career politician, which many voters saw as a plus.

Republican gubernatorial candidate Norm Coleman waits for his wife, Laurie, shortly after he voted in the November 3, 1998, election.

As in his campaign for mayor, Ventura drew volunteers new to politics or the Reform Party. People such as Dolphin Engstrom, one of his first supporters, who says:

> I was a Democrat all my life, but they didn't have anything to say to me this time, so I worked for the campaign, and I felt like part of something bigger than myself, and the other parties never made me feel that way. We were the only people who seemed to be having any fun.[92]

Ventura's campaign slogan was an aggressive "Retaliate In '98," but having fun was Ventura's top priority, a concept that extended to his campaign ads. One television spot featured a Ventura action figure battling special interests and growling, "I don't want your stupid money."[93] Another posed Ventura as Rodin's statue, *The Thinker*. The candidate, who appeared to be nude while the camera slowly revolved around him, gave a big wink at the end.

In a series of six debates, Ventura won the respect of voters by combining straight talk on issues—he was unafraid to support gun ownership, gay rights, and abortion rights—with a tough demeanor, quirky sense of humor, and solid jabs at his opponents. "I'm the only candidate," Ventura says, "that's spent his entire career literally working in the private sector. Even while I was mayor I was required to hold a full time job in the private sector. My two opponents, they've been cashing government checks for well over twenty years."[94] His stinging criticism of their long government careers left both fighting to defend themselves.

It was a low budget, low key campaign in which Ventura raised money by selling T-shirts. He said he would lower taxes, give the surplus back to taxpayers, reduce government involvement in the lives of residents, increase the quality of education (he selected retired school teacher Mae Schunk as his lieutenant governor), and stressed that he was an average person, the only candidate who was a member of a union, the Screen Actors Guild.

Ventura was at his most effective greeting people one-on-one. At the Minnesota State Fair he raised money and courted voters by sitting in a booth and answering their every question, even why he had changed his nickname. "I make my living with my mind now

Why Jesse Ventura Won

Jesse Ventura's election as governor of Minnesota shocked the political establishment. Here are several commentaries on why he won:

In *The Nation* magazine, Michah I. Sifry says Ventura was elected because voters rejected the two major party candidates:

> Third political parties win when the major parties fail. First and foremost, people vote third-party as a protest against the failure of the major parties to reflect their concerns.

In *Time* magazine, humorist Garrison Keillor speculates that many people voted for Ventura to spite the traditional parties but never thought he would win:

> He was the protest candidate, a chance to throw toilet paper in the trees and piss off Dad, nobody dreaming he would actually be elected. But in a three-way race, the ball takes funny bounces, and that is how Minnesota got a 6 ft. 4 in., 250-lb. governor named Jesse ("The Body") Ventura, and all week [after the election] Minnesotans were feeling sort of giddy about it. Who woulda thunk we could get this crazy? He ran a smart race, snarled, boasted, was entertaining, campaigned in a sweatshirt ("Retaliate in '98"), sat in on the televised debates with his two opponents (who didn't bother to mess with him), but kept saying he was no politician and expressed himself more bluntly than had been customary in Minnesota politics. He cussed a little. He was vaguely outrageous, the right thing to be when you're running against two suits.

In *Time* magazine, Paul Gray explained Ventura's victory this way:

> Boredom seems to be the most likely answer, plus a growing grass-roots resentment of elitist politicians who govern by focus groups rather than personal convictions. Says Steven Schier, chairman of the political-science department at Minnesota's Carleton College, of Ventura: "He's charismatic, he's warm, he's colorful. [Republican] Coleman and [Democrat] Humphrey were much more conventional politicians and provided a nice gray backdrop. Every act needs a straight man, and he had two of them." Ventura's campaign manager, Doug Friedline, says, "He's very straightforward and honest. You may not like his answers, but you're gonna get them anyway."

Even his wrestling nemesis, Hulk Hogan, had an opinion:

> Jesse's victory proves that people want a real man in power to lead, not a play plastic puppet like other politicians.

Jesse Ventura supporters celebrate joyously as he is declared the winner of the Minnesota gubernatorial race. The victory that "shocked the world" delighted his backers.

instead of my body, so I'm Jesse 'The Mind,'" he said. Asked whether that would disappoint his wrestling fans, he joked, "I don't think so, because I still have eighteen-inch pipes [biceps]."[95]

Ventura moved up in the polls and campaigned even harder, spending the last seventy-two hours before election day touring the state in a recreational vehicle. "I remember pulling into Willmar [a small town in western Minnesota]," Ventura recalls. "There were about 600 people waiting there in the middle of night in a parking lot, going crazy. One young kid, 18 or 19 years old, yelled out, 'Jesse! Remember: You are us!'"[96]

The result of Ventura's intense campaigning was that on election night, he finished with 37 percent of the votes (768,356) to defeat Coleman, who was second with 35 percent, and Humphrey, who garnered 28 percent. Ventura had made voters believe an average person, someone without a college degree but with common sense and street smarts developed from years of struggling to support his family, could govern Minnesota.

Chapter 6

Jesse "The Governor" Ventura

Jesse Ventura was as surprised as anyone November 3, 1998, when Minnesota voters elected him governor. Terry remembers how shocked they were while vote totals indicating his victory rolled across the television screen at his election night headquarters:

> We sat watching TV with our mouths open. And we cracked open a bottle of champagne and drank it all, and stayed up until 4 A.M. We laughed, we cried, we kept pointing to each other and going, "You're the governor," and, "You're the first lady," and "Oh, my God."[97]

Ventura had maintained during the campaign that the only legal requirements for governor were to be twenty-five years old and have resided in the state for a year. "That's what the Founding Fathers wanted,"[98] Ventura said, arguing that an average person should be able to become governor. In a humorous attempt to bolster that claim, Ventura was fond of remarking, "I don't find a lot of elected officials to be all that bright."[99]

But the day after Ventura became the first Reform Party candidate in the nation elected to statewide office, he was faced with the task of actually governing Minnesota. It was the biggest challenge of his life, and even Ventura acknowledged a few months later that the job was more difficult than he had ever imagined:

> Ever since that check mark went next to my name at 11:55 P.M. on election night, it's been like being in a rubber raft

in a river with a current so fast that you can't paddle against it. You just go with it."[100]

Jesse Takes Office

When Ventura was sworn in January 4, 1999, he signed his official oath of office "James G. Janos, AKA [also known as] Jesse Ventura." Donning a size 50 business suit instead of his customary fringed leather jacket, Ventura candidly stated in his inaugural speech that he would make mistakes but promised, "I will do the best job I possibly can to the best of my ability."[101] His inaugural celebration two weeks later for fifteen thousand supporters at the Target Center, a sports arena in downtown Minneapolis, was more to his style, a wild bash that featured music by Warren Zevon. Clad in a Jimi Hendrix T-shirt, bandanna, feather boa, and earrings, the governor sang a duet with Zevon to the hit song "Werewolves of London." When the music died, he went back to being Jesse "The Governor" Ventura.

Ventura's first challenge was to appoint a personal staff and select commissioners to head state agencies and advise him on policy matters. It was important for a beginner like Ventura to surround himself with experienced, capable people, and he received high marks for his appointees, chosen from the Democratic and Republican Parties as well as from his own Reform Party. Some political observers claimed it was the most talented cabinet in two decades, and Ventura was even backhandedly complimented by Al Quie, a former Minnesota governor who had questioned whether Ventura could do the job. "I'm less worried as time goes by," Quie said, "because of the people he's appointed so far. Put in quality people, and you can get away with a lot of ineptitude."[102]

Ventura's Accomplishments

From the beginning, the Ventura administration had a humanistic style, one that is summed up by quotations adorning the home page of the governor's website: "There are no dumb questions," "You can't legislate against stupidity," "Every vote counts," and "Love is bigger than government." Ventura's political philosophy is a blend of liberalism on social issues—he

Looking more like a rock star than a governor, Jesse Ventura celebrates his election victory in style at a huge party at the Target Center in Minneapolis.

backs gay rights and abortion rights—and conservatism on government affairs, fiscal restraint and a belief in individual responsibility. He also believes government should play a limited role in peoples' lives:

> I believe government should only do for you what you can't do for yourself, to do things for the common good that you as an individual can't. You as an individual can't build a highway, so therefore it's government's role to build those roads so we can all use them for the common good.[103]

Thanks to a booming economy that produced a $1.3 billion budget surplus, Ventura was able to mastermind what his aides said was the largest tax rebate in American history. Taxpayers received an average check of $630 in the form of a sales tax rebate, a technicality Ventura initiated to prevent the federal government from taxing it again. He proudly noted that Minnesotans called their rebates "Jesse checks" and said, "They found out I could govern almost as well as I could wrestle."[104] A $525 million budget surplus in 2000 enabled Minnesota to return more money to residents. Even though checks were only about half the size of those in 1999, they helped keep Ventura's popularity high.

In his first year Ventura also made good on his pledge to boost state funding for education and to cut state taxes. But in creating a budget, the rookie governor discovered how hard it is to hold down spending:

> The most basic thing I've realized is that it's easy for everyone to holler for tax cuts, but in government, the law of physics prevails. I only got Cs in physics classes, but I do remember the basic principle: For every action, there's an equal and opposite reaction. When people say cut taxes, they have to understand that you can't do it without cutting spending.[105]

Ventura Versus the Legislature

A governor, however, can only propose programs. It is the Legislature that makes those ideas into law, and Ventura had problems dealing with the Minnesota House and Senate. There were two main reasons for Ventura's sometimes awkward political dance with lawmakers: He was not a career politician or member of either the Republican or Democratic parties they belonged to and, as a political novice, he did not know how to work with them to accomplish what he wanted. Dave Jennings, a former Republican House Speaker who served briefly in the Ventura administration, said Ventura is hard for many veteran lawmakers to understand:

> He doesn't care if he gets re-elected. His life doesn't revolve around politics or political office. Unlike some elected officials who are mindful not just of this office but the next, and not just of this election but the next, this guy doesn't think that way. That changes all the rules.[106]

Members of the Legislature have complained that Ventura has not tried to forge a real partnership with them. The governor blindsided the Legislature by using his line item veto to strip $160 million worth of programs in his first budget. The vetoes stunned legislators, who had worked hard with the governor's office to craft deals on the programs and helped Ventura secure votes to fund his light-rail transit proposal. Ventura also angered lawmakers by adorning his vetoes with a red pig stamp, his way of symbolically terming the spending provisions as pork, a term for wasteful spending.

Ashley Grant, the lead government reporter for the Associated Press in Minnesota, said relations between the legislative and executive branches have been strained at times because Ventura did not know how to interact with legislators:

> The governor has had a few stumbles with lawmakers. Some people have said he isn't as engaged as he should be in state politics because he does not attend many legislative committee hearings. The two sides have not always been friendly and at times he has called them "gutless cowards" for not acting on his proposals.[107]

Governor Jesse Ventura and his advisers confer with Minnesota state legislators. Ventura has clashed often with members of the Legislature over a variety of issues.

> ## An Old SEAL Returns Home
> One of Jesse Ventura's proudest appearances as governor occurred in July 1999 when he spoke to a graduating class of SEALs at the Coronado Naval Amphibious Base in San Diego, where he had trained. His visit was chronicled by Gidget Fuentes in the *Navy Times:*
>> It took an election victory for a former Navy storekeeper third class to get the salutes of military officers. It's one perk of being Minnesota governor that Jesse Ventura just won't pass up. Ventura, a former SEAL and Vietnam-era veteran, spent two days visiting his old barracks at the Coronado Naval Amphibious Base and helping close out the dreaded "Hell Week" of SEAL training. "The only way to become governor is to become an enlisted man," said Ventura, speaking July 30 to a dinner crowd of mostly enlisted military service members and their dates at the Loews Coronado Bay Resort. . . . Military service is "truly the barometer of my life," he told them. "It makes you grow up. It makes you accept responsibility." He hailed the contributions of enlisted military people, "the backbone of the United States military. I can happily say that I was one."

One of those "gutless" claims came in his second year, when legislators refused to consider his tradition-shattering proposal to switch to a unicameral, or one house Legislature (Nebraska is the only state that has a unicameral system). Ventura believes the two-house system, patterned after Congress, leads to negative partisan politics and allows a few veteran legislators to wield too much power in conference committees, which meet to reconcile differences in bills the two houses have passed.

Ventura gradually came to realize there was little he could do to control the Legislature except to cooperate more with lawmakers. There was something else he found out he had no power over—the effect his new position had on his wife and children.

The First Family

Ventura's election took away his family's privacy. "I didn't realize how overwhelmingly it would affect them," he admitted. "Now my kids have bodyguards."[108] Long accustomed to dealing with his own celebrity, even Ventura found that his new fame and power could be unsettling. "You become a slave," he said. "I can't go anywhere without guards. You become a prisoner of your own success."[109] But there were also benefits for members of Minnesota's First Family.

His son, Tyrel, joked at first that his dad's new job might help him get more dates. More importantly, his status as "first son" opened doors in the film world for the aspiring director. After meeting actors Jack Nicholson and Sean Penn in February 1999 when they visited the governor's mansion, Tyrel spent four months in early 2000 working as an assistant to Penn while Penn directed a movie. Tyrel, who made his acting debut in his dad's 1989 movie *Thunderground*, also was chosen to direct his father in a 1999 commercial for Minnesota colleges and universities. "The door will be cracked open [because of his name]," Tyrel

Tyrel Ventura stands to the right of actor Sean Penn and actress Virginie Ledoyen at the Cannes Film Festival in France on May 18, 2000. Being the governor's son gave Tyrel the chance to meet and work with Penn.

acknowledges, "but then no matter who you are, you have to perform or you have to get out of the room."[110]

The news media loved interviewing the handsome, articulate Tyrel but kept its distance from Jade, a shy high school student who struggles at times to fit in because of her disabilities. However, some good for children like Jade came out of the family's new prominence when Jesse and Terry set up the Jade Foundation to help disadvantaged children. In May 2000 the group raised $80,000 with a concert, an event that included a reception with Minnesota's famous First Family.

The media spotlight shone most brightly on Terry, who was unaccustomed to being interviewed by national magazines or performing the public duties required of an elected official's wife. "I'm not like the other First Ladies with fourteen million college degrees and a husband who was groomed to be a politician," she says, "but I do have common sense. If I just use that common sense and don't step on any toes, then I think it will work out fine."[111] Although the family lives in the executive mansion, she continues to run her horse-training business on the family ranch in Maple Grove.

Governor Jesse Ventura takes time from his busy schedule to have dinner with his family.

Leaving the Reform Party

On February 11, 2000, Governor Jesse Ventura decided to quit the Reform Party and re-establish the Independence Party of Minnesota, its predecessor. The move thrust Ventura into the national spotlight and made him an even more powerful player in the 2000 presidential election. The move did not affect his status as governor; it was basically a name change for a political organization he controlled. One reason for leaving was that he disagreed with the philosophy of the expected Reform Party presidential candidate, Pat Buchanan. Here are excerpts from a letter Ventura wrote to Reform Party members:

> Having watched the national Reform Party in recent months, I have concluded that it is best for the Reform Party of Minnesota to disaffiliate from the national Reform Party and reclaim its original Independence Party name. . . . Based on what I have seen in prior years and especially in recent months, I have come to believe that the national Reform Party is hopelessly dysfunctional. It is unworthy of my support and the support of the American people. . . . I'm also recommending disaffiliation and a name change for ideological reasons. Pat Buchanan is now a figure in the Reform Party and is virtually unopposed in the quest for the Reform Party nomination. Buchanan is an anti-abortion extremist and unrealistic isolationist. The Minnesota Reform Party is the party of the political center. In Minnesota, we cannot maintain our socially moderate identity while a right-winger heads our national ticket. If we are to win state and local elections in Minnesota, we must stick to our proven success formula. We must continue to stand as fiscal conservatives and social moderates.

Ventura's schedule is demanding, but he made a commitment to devote Sundays to family activities, warning his staff not to interrupt him unless there is an emergency. Jesse and Terry steal time together by exercising every morning on treadmills and she cooks family dinners whenever possible. Evenings when Ventura is free usually are quiet. "By the end of the day," Ventura says, "I enjoy putting my feet up, watching the mindless box for a little while."[112] Sometimes, Ventura even finds time to play with his pet bulldog, Franklin.

Those restful times, however, are few. In addition to governing Minnesota, he is still busy making as much money as he can to support his family.

Making Money as Governor

Ventura boasted once of his money-making prowess: "One month of the royalties from the Jesse 'The Body' action figure bought me a red Porsche. I'm a capitalist. I've been obsessed with earning a living and going out and working hard my whole life."[113]

As governor, he continued to do that with a vengeance. The Minneapolis *Star Tribune* estimates that in 1999, Ventura earned $2 million to $3 million, a sum that dwarfed his governor's salary of $120,000. Money flowed in from the sale of action figures (Ventura as either a Navy SEAL, football coach, or governor), his advance for his best-selling *I Ain't Got Time to Bleed* (he received an additional $100,000 in 2000 for an updated paperback version), and a return to the ring August 22, 1999, as a guest referee for a World Wrestling Federation pay-per-view telecast.

Although Ventura donated $100,000 of his fee to charity in a vain attempt to quiet the uproar over a governor being linked with wrestling, it is believed he could earn as much as $1 million from video sales. However, profits from the sale of action figures and other items marketed by a nonprofit group he organized, Ventura for Minnesota Inc., are donated to charity.

When Ventura was elected, he vowed not to do anything to cheapen the office of governor: "I'm not going to turn it into some dog-and-pony show."[114] But his pursuit of money led to charges that he was cashing in on his position as governor. Doug Spong, a managing partner in a Minneapolis-based public relations firm, claimed:

> People saw not just Jesse the Governor, but Jesse the Brand, and started asking, was he serving us as governor, or were we serving him in terms of his fortune? Every day that he wakes up, the first thought in his head is not 'What can I do to serve the people in Minnesota?' but 'What can I do for Jesse?'"[115]

The wrestling event that Ventura guest-refereed was held in Minneapolis, and when he entered the ring, he told wrestlers, "You're in my state now, I am law and order here."[116] The phrase angered some Minnesotans—How could his power as governor be transferred to policing a wrestling match?—as did Ventura's swearing during the telecast. But the ill-chosen phrases were only a few of many missteps the man once nicknamed "The Mouth" would make during his first year as governor.

Jesse "The Brand" Ventura

Ventura's decision to continue selling himself even after being elected governor was the topic of a story in the November 1999 issue of *Corporate Report–Minnesota*. John Rosengren detailed Ventura's money-making prowess and the governor's defense of his right to profit while in office:

> You've known him as the Body, the Mouth and, fleetingly, the Mind; now meet Jesse the Brand. Throughout his ascent, Jesse Ventura has shown entrepreneurial chutzpah and self-promotional savvy in peddling his image for profit. Although already a millionaire when he entered office, his stint as Minnesota's governor has proven to be the most lucrative enterprise of his life. He's proven himself a whiz kid in the ability to package himself. James Janos—the governor's legal name—recast himself as Jesse Ventura years ago, then trademarked and licensed his name and image in the early '80s. "I'm entrepreneuring myself," the governor says. "Jesse Ventura is my product. I am able to sell Jesse Ventura as the commodity he is." Ventura admits that holding the state's highest elected office has helped him personally. "I'm sure it has," he says. "Anyone would be lying to say it didn't."
>
> [Ventura has been attacked by some for using the post to make money but he] counters that he's criticized only by the media and defends his moonlighting as patriotic. "I only get heat from the media," he says. "The average citizen doesn't hold against me the fact that I want to go out and entrepreneur myself. Holding down a second job is very American. Having a business on the side is as basic American as apple pie."

Governor Jesse Ventura is introduced at the World Wrestling Federation's SummerSlam *event in Minneapolis, August 22, 1999.*

Controversial Remarks

Ventura once commented, "My brain is operating at such a level that I don't want to put my foot in it."[117] But that is just what he kept doing, over and over. During a February 23, 1999, appearance on *Late Night with David Letterman*, the conversation turned unexpectedly to the idiosyncratic layout of St. Paul's streets. Ventura commented facetiously, "Whoever designed the streets must have been drunk. . . . I think it was those Irish guys."[118] Although he later apologized, it was a careless, cutting comment that inflamed Minnesotans of Irish descent. Publication of *I Ain't Got Time to Bleed* in 1999 had created a furor because of Ventura's admissions that when he was younger he took steroids to bulk up his body, smoked marijuana, and hired prostitutes.

Ventura got into more trouble when a long interview in the November 1999 issue of *Playboy* magazine delved further into

The Infamous *Playboy* Interview

Probably the most damaging thing Jesse Ventura did in his first year as governor was to make intemperate, some would say bone-headed, comments in the November 1999 edition of *Playboy* magazine. He infuriated many people by sounding arrogant while making controversial statements in a long interview with Lawrence Grobel. The following quotes are from the article; the question is first, followed by his answer:

What's the best thing about being governor? It's good to be the king. The best thing is that there's no one in this state who can tell me what to do.

Why do so many people kill other people with guns? Because it's an easy tool to use. If that tool were eliminated they would use something else. There weren't guns when Cain killed Abel. You want to know my definition of gun control? Being able to stand there at 25 meters and put two rounds in the same hole. That's gun control. The gun control people don't know what they're talking about.

[Legalizing prostitution, which Ventura backs] isn't a very popular position in America, is it? No, and it's because of religion. Organized religion is a sham and a crutch for weak-minded people who need strength in numbers. It tells people to go out and stick their noses in other people's business. I live by the golden rule: Treat others as you'd want them to treat you. The religious right wants to tell people how to live.

[Referring to his military duty] Have you ever killed anyone? You don't ask a question like that—it's inappropriate. That's no one's business.

those claims about his early life and included controversial remarks on other topics, including his belief that organized religion was for the weak-minded. In the updated paperback version of *I Ain't Got Time to Bleed,* published in June 2000, Ventura tried to explain away the controversy by claiming he was referring to the so-called religious right, conservatives who are active in politics, and that he did not mean to demean people who believe in religion:

> I don't have any problem with the vast majority of religious folks. I count myself among them, more or less. But I believe because it makes sense to me, not because I think it can be proven. I don't think any of the stuff religion has to say can be proven—true or false.[119]

In May 1999 Ventura caused another stir when commenting on the tragic shooting at Columbine High School in Colorado. A hunter and gun-rights advocate, he said, "To me, it justifies conceal and carry more."[120] Ventura reasoned that if other people inside the school had been carrying guns, they could have defended the unarmed students who died. The comment infuriated people who believe easy access to guns was partly to blame for the incident.

In December 1999, *People* named Ventura one of the year's twenty-five most intriguing people. But the magazine also noted his penchant for making stupid comments:

> It's the talking, not the governing, that has kept the former James George Janos in the national spotlight. Steven Schier, a professor of political science at Minnesota's Carleton College, says that Ventura "puts his foot in his mouth and refuses to take it out. It's extraordinary for a politician to make such mistakes." But as Ventura's popularity both in Minnesota and elsewhere continues to float at robust levels, it may be that the mistake is being made by professional politics watchers like Schier. "I could never be a career politician," says Ventura, "because I believe in telling the truth."[121]

A FBI SWAT team waits outside Columbine High School in Littleton, Colorado. Governor Jesse Ventura created a controversy with some ill-advised comments about the tragic shooting deaths of students there in 1999.

When Ventura told what he saw as the truth, the news media was only too happy to report it. But after his comments started getting him into trouble, he began a running battle with reporters.

Jesse Versus the Media

One of the skirmishes occurred at a Minnesota Timberwolves basketball game when reporters peppered him with questions about the negative response to his autobiographical revelations about his early years. "You're asking me to apologize for my life," he told them angrily. "Is that what you're asking me to do?" The next day at a news conference, however, Ventura was almost apologetic. "I am your governor," he said, "and all I ask is that you judge me on my ability to govern." [122]

Like all politicians, Ventura loves the news media when they praise him and hates the media when they criticize him or produce stories he feels are negative. Ventura claims he has trouble with reporters because they don't know when he is joking:

I think the big problem with the mainstream media is, they have no sense of humor. When you do something tongue in cheek after you're elected, they usually think it's inappropriate. My message to them is, I will have fun whether they like it or not. We all support freedom of the press and speech, but with that comes responsibility, which the media tends to shirk in many ways. When there is no news, they often attempt to create it in the spin they try to put on stories. That shouldn't be their role; they need to just report the news as it is. The media also attempts to control government decisions by using editorial influence, which is dangerous.[123]

Ventura's remarks seem to suggest that he does not understand that it is the media's duty to report whatever he says, whether the comments are smart, dumb, or even libelous, and it is his responsibility not to say things that might get him into trouble.

Off to a Good Start

Despite his verbal gaffes, Ventura's first eighteen months in office were positive and he has generally received high marks for his work; even Tim Pawlenty, the Minnesota House majority leader with

Attacking the News Media

An updated paperback version of *I Ain't Got Time to Bleed* was published in June 2000. The new material detailing Jesse Ventura's first year as governor includes several comments critical of the news media. In a May 25, 2000, story in the Minneapolis *Star Tribune*, Conrad deFiebre previewed the governor's anti-media message:

> With "a few honorable exceptions," Ventura says . . . the media are "corrupt, shameless and irresponsible as hell." [His] experiences "with the local press constantly nipping at my heels" have made Ventura "more cautious about the way I phrase things," he writes. Elsewhere in the chapter, however, he says, "I'm stubborn enough to keep speaking my mind anyway" and "I'm never going to be politically correct." Ventura takes the Minnesota media to task for "making me look as a bad as possible" and "creating scandal where none exists." He writes: "They misquoted me, they took my words out of context and they . . . love to put an ugly spin on anything I do."

whom he has clashed, concedes the governor deserves at least a B-plus. Ashley Grant, who has been writing about Ventura since his gubernatorial campaign, acknowledges that Ventura has done some good things but notes, "I think the first thing to recognize is that he started out with a big advantage, the Minnesota economy was in great shape with record employment. Anyone who stepped into that situation should have done well." [124]

Grant also said that some of the problems Ventura has had because of intemperate remarks and poor relations with lawmakers have eased. "He's more toned down," she said in June 2000. "He is not a lifelong politician, so he's sort of been learning as he goes along." [125]

Epilogue

Jesse "The President" Ventura?

JESSE VENTURA HAS spent his entire life refining and redefining himself. "I've reinvented myself a couple of times," he says. "That's just like improving your product. If you don't improve yourself, you're going to get left behind."[126] The stages of his life can be categorized easily, if somewhat simplistically, by their attendant name changes. The big switch was from James George Janos to Jesse Ventura when he began wrestling, but the former Navy SEAL known as "Janos the Dirty" has collected a number of shifting nicknames: "The Body," "The Mouth," and now "The Mind."

After his election as governor, some national publications tried to anoint Ventura with a more prestigious, unlikely title—that of "political prophet." The powerful appeal Ventura displayed in motivating young people and others who had been too bored with politics to vote led to the kind of lavish editorial praise typified by this comment from Kenneth T. Walsh in *U.S. News & World Report*: "His startling ascension as the nation's second independent governor [the other was Angus King of Maine] may be a glimpse at a new kind of state politics, a true 'third way' that body-slams the old preconceptions."[127]

Even though Ventura was not a member of their political parties, his reputation in early 2000 led Democratic Vice President Al Gore and Republican Arizona Senator John McCain to journey to Minnesota to seek his endorsement, and any votes his support might bring to their presidential campaigns. A June 5 *Newsweek* magazine story titled "Wrestling For

Governor Jesse Ventura and Vice President Al Gore visit Hopkins North Junior High School in June 2000. Ventura claims that Gore is a much more interesting and humorous person than his public demeanor indicates.

The Center" even claimed that to win the presidential election, a candidate would need to flash Ventura-like appeal to independent voters. Reporter Matt Bai asked the governor how candidates could do that:

> I guess I would tell them to be themselves, but I don't know if they're capable of doing that. They're too rehearsed. They're too spun [worried about how voters

will react to what they say]. They're who their parties think they should be to win. And now their parties are gonna' try to spin them to be me.[128]

Ventura, however, has never had any trouble being himself, even if that image is one he has carefully crafted. When Ventura gave his first national press conference at a governors' meeting in Delaware, he wore a fringed buckskin jacket and pointed snakeskin boots. Asked by an adviser why he didn't wear a suit, he said, "I just decided to give 'em what they want."[129] "The Mind" was smart enough to realize that his eccentric attire would generate more stories and headlines than a plain blue suit ever could.

Ventura himself was even mentioned as a possible presidential candidate, speculation that increased in February 2000 after he withdrew from the Reform Party and regenerated the Independence Party, Reform's predecessor in Minnesota. Although Ventura denied he would seek the presidency, as late as June he told a national magazine, "I still believe strongly that I could walk in and steal this election at the 11th hour. It was sort of scary, how many people were begging me to run."[130]

But Schier, chairman of the political science program at Carleton College in Northfield, Minnesota, believes Ventura was only acting out the part he has scripted for himself for so many years. Ventura, he says, was simply promoting himself:

> Why should he put this [speculation] to sleep? His job is being famous, and I can't think of a better way to keep his name in circulation than to be discussed by the great mentioners. It's marketing, and he's great at marketing.[131]

Selling Jesse

Many people consider Ventura's constant drive to make money inappropriate for an elected official, with some even questioning whether he ran only to make himself more marketable, win or lose. Even Ventura backers recognize his combination of politics and profits is unprecedented. "No other sitting politician has ever had an action figure," says David Bradley Olsen, Ventura's personal attorney and one of four Ventura for Minnesota Inc. board members. "No other sitting politician has ever marketed consumer-type items the way we are."[132]

Ventura's ceaseless self-promotion clouds his political future, as does his flippant manner with the media; he often changes his mind on issues, making it hard to gauge what he really means. But a comment in *George* magazine in 1999 indicated that he viewed the governorship as simply another phase in his constantly evolving celebrity career: "I think I've been successful in just about every endeavor I've gone into—and there's been a lot. I don't hold jobs long. That's why politics might work perfect for me. It's four years, then you're on to a new job, baby."[133]

Although Ventura's popularity remained high through the first half of his first term, he was hesitant about committing to run for another four years as governor. His personal indecision, coupled with his many extracurricular activities, including an appearance in June 2000 on *The Young and the Restless,* his favorite television soap opera, raised doubts about whether he would remain in politics or return to the private sector. Ventura

Governor-elect Jesse Ventura answers questions at a news conference the day after his stunning victory. Smiling behind him is outgoing governor Arne Carlson.

has bragged, for example, about how much he could earn on the lecture circuit when he leaves office.

Ventura also continued his talk show exploits with a weekly show that delved into politics and other issues. Only now, as governor, he was commenting from inside the political process, as when he attacked high gasoline prices in June 2000. His comments were as volatile as ever, only now they carried far greater weight: "We should inquire as to why gas prices are being raped and pillaged, and I'll use that word over in the Midwest here. Why are the prices soaring in the Midwest and they're not soaring everywhere else?"[134]

Ventura's Future

Although Ventura's immediate future was uncertain in 2000, he already has his retirement planned. When *Minneapolis-St. Paul Magazine* asked what he thought he would be doing in the year 2015, he responded:

> I see myself living on a beach somewhere. Riding a surfboard. Not owning a watch. Knowing that when the sun comes up you get up, when it's straight overhead you eat lunch, and when it goes down you go to bed. This is more than a dream. It will happen because I can make it happen. I'm purposefully keeping my head shaved because when I leave office I'm going to let my hair grow out and grow a beard so I'll be unrecognizable. I'm also in the process of changing what my body's going to look like—I'm back to my swimming and hope to eventually get down to 210 or 220 pounds. If I'm tall and thin and have a beard and long hair, I'm sure I won't be recognized.[135]

Notes

Introduction: The Many Faces of Jesse Ventura
1. Quoted in inaugural speech by Jesse Ventura, January 4, 1999. Minnesota State Government website, www.mainserver.state.mn.us/governor/inaugural_speech.html.
2. Quoted in *A&E Biography,* "Body Slam Week: Jesse Ventura, The Body Politic," Nov. 18, 1999.
3. Quoted in Ventura inaugural speech, Minnesota State Government website.
4. Quoted in Ventura inaugural speech, Minnesota State Government website.
5. Quoted in Ventura inaugural speech, Minnesota State Government website.

Chapter 1: James George Janos
6. Quoted in *A&E Biography,* "Body Slam Week: Jesse Ventura, The Body Politic."
7. Quoted in transcript of Internet interview conducted May 27, 1999, on the Barnes & Noble website, shop.barnesandnoble.com.
8. Quoted in Kevin Dockery and Bill Fawcett, *The Teams: An Oral History of the U.S. Navy SEALs.* New York: William Morrow and Company, Inc., 1998, p. 220.
9. Quoted in Dockery and Fawcett, *The Teams,* p. 220.
10. Quoted in *A&E Biography,* "Body Slam Week: Jesse Ventura, The Body Politic."
11. Jesse Ventura, *I Ain't Got Time to Bleed: Reworking the Body Politic From the Bottom Up.* New York: Villard, 1999, p. 44.

Notes

12. Ventura, *I Ain't Got Time to Bleed*, pp. 42–43.
13. Jake Tapper, *Body Slam: The Jesse Ventura Story*. New York: St. Martin's Paperbacks, 1999, p. 9.
14. Quoted in *A&E Biography*, "Body Slam Week: Jesse Ventura, The Body Politic."
15. Quoted in Kermit Pattison, "Pinning Jesse Down," *George*, March 1999, p. 92+.
16. Tapper, *Body Slam*, p. 10.
17. Quoted in *A&E Biography*, "Body Slam Week: Jesse Ventura, The Body Politic."
18. Quoted in Britt Robson, "The Body Politic," *City Pages*, September 30, 1998, p. 1+.
19. Ventura, *I Ain't Got Time to Bleed*, p. 49.
20. Ventura, *I Ain't Got Time to Bleed*, p. 49.
21. Quoted in Tapper, *Body Slam*, p. 14.
22. Quoted in Tapper, *Body Slam*, p. 14.
23. Quoted in *A&E Biography*, "Body Slam Week: Jesse Ventura, The Body Politic."
24. Quoted in Robson, "The Body Politic," p. 1+.

Chapter 2: Janos "The Dirty"

25. Ventura, *I Ain't Got Time to Bleed*, p. 51.
26. Quoted in Dockery and Fawcett, *The Teams*, p. 223.
27. Quoted in Dockery and Fawcett, *The Teams*, p. 224.
28. Quoted in *A&E Biography*, "Body Slam Week: Jesse Ventura, The Body Politic."
29. Ventura, *I Ain't Got Time to Bleed*, p. 232.
30. Quoted in Richard J. Newman and Rick Rickman, "Tougher Than Hell," *U.S. News & World Report*, November 3, 1997, p. 42+.
31. Ventura, *I Ain't Got Time to Bleed*, p. 69.
32. Quoted in Robson, "The Body Politic," p. 1+.
33. Quoted in Dockery and Fawcett, *The Teams*, p. 224.
34. Quoted in Robson, "The Body Politic," p. 1+.
35. Quoted in Dockery and Fawcett, *The Teams*, p. xiii.
36. Quoted in Tapper, *Body Slam*, p. 27.
37. Ventura, *I Ain't Got Time to Bleed*, p. 78.

38. Quoted in Tapper, *Body Slam*, p. 34.
39. Quoted in Robson, "The Body Politic," p. 1+.
40. Quoted in Dockery and Fawcett, *The Teams*, p. 283.

Chapter 3: Jesse "The Body" Ventura

41. Quoted in Jessica Allen, *The Wit and Wisdom of Jesse "The Body . . . The Mind" Ventura*. New York: William Morrow and Company, Inc., 1999, p. 15.
42. Quoted in Dockery and Fawcett, *The Teams*, p. 282.
43. Quoted in Paul Gray, "Body Slam," *Time*, November 16, 1998, p. 56.
44. Quoted in Dockery and Fawcett, *The Teams*, p. 282.
45. Quoted in Tapper, *Body Slam*, p. 40.
46. Quoted in Kathy O'Malley, "The Reluctant First Lady," *McCall's*, July 1999, p. 63.
47. Quoted in *A&E Biography*, " Body Slam Week: Jesse Ventura, The Body Politic."
48. Quoted in Tapper, *Body Slam*, p. 47.
49. Ventura, *I Ain't Got Time to Bleed*, p. 93.
50. Quoted in Allen, *The Wit and Wisdom of Jesse "The Body . . . The Mind" Ventura*, p. 4.
51. Quoted in "Jesse Ventura," *Current Biography*, May 1999, p. 54.
52. Quoted in Matt Bai and David Brauer, "Jesse Ventura's 'Body' Politics," *Newsweek*, November 16, 1998, p. 40.
53. Quoted in *A&E Biography*, "Body Slam Week: Jesse Ventura, The Body Politic."
54. Quoted in Lawrence Grobel, "Playboy Interview: Jesse Ventura." *Playboy*, November 1999, p. 55+.
55. Ventura, *I Ain't Got Time to Bleed*, p. 91.
56. Quoted in Charles P. Pierce, "The First Hundred Hours," *Esquire*, April 1999, p. 104.
57. Quoted in Richard Leiby, "I'm Not Like Other First Ladies," *Good Housekeeping*, August 1999, p. 29+.
58. Quoted in *A&E Biography*, " Body Slam Week: Jesse Ventura, The Body Politic,"
59. Quoted in Allen, *The Wit and Wisdom of Jesse "The Body . . . The Mind" Ventura*, p. 22.

60. Quoted in Allen, *The Wit and Wisdom of Jesse "The Body . . . The Mind" Ventura*, p. 22.
61. Tapper, *Body Slam*, p. 60.

Chapter 4: Jesse "The Mouth" Ventura

62. Quoted in Robson, "The Body Politic," p. 1+.
63. Ventura, *I Ain't Got Time to Bleed*, p. 114.
64. Quoted in "Jesse Ventura," *Current Biography*, p. 55.
65. Quoted in Pierce, "The First Hundred Hours," p. 104.
66. Quoted in Tapper, *Body Slam*, p. 69.
67. Quoted in Grobel, "Playboy Interview: Jesse Ventura," p. 55+.
68. Ventura, *I Ain't Got Time to Bleed*, p. 125.
69. Quoted in Roger Ebert, "The Running Man," *Chicago Sun-Times*, November 13, 1987.
70. Quoted in review of *Abraxas, Guardian of the Universe*, Amazing World of Cult Movies Internet site, www.awcm.com.
71. Ventura, *I Ain't Got Time to Bleed*, pp. 135–36.
72. Quoted in Tapper, *Body Slam*, p. 80.
73. Quoted in Tapper, *Body Slam*, p. 129.
74. Quoted in Robson, "The Body Politic," p. 1+.
75. Ventura, *I Ain't Got Time to Bleed*, pp. 154–55.
76. Quoted in Tapper, *Body Slam*, p. 130.

Chapter 5: Jesse "The Mayor" Ventura

77. Ventura, *I Ain't Got Time to Bleed*, p. 45.
78. Quoted in *A&E Biography*, " Body Slam Week: Jesse Ventura, The Body Politic."
79. Quoted in Pattison, "Pinning Jesse Down," p. 92+.
80. Quoted in Leiby, "I'm Not Like Other First Ladies," p. 29+.
81. Ventura, *I Ain't Got Time to Bleed*, p. 145.
82. Quoted in Pattison, "Pinning Jesse Down," p. 92+.
83. Quoted in Robson, "The Body Politic," p. 1+.
84. Quoted in O'Malley, "The Reluctant First Lady," p. 62.
85. Quoted in Robson, "The Body Politic," p. 1+.
86. Quoted in Allen, *The Wit and Wisdom of Jesse "The Body . . . The Mind" Ventura*, p. 30.

87. Quoted in Gray, "Body Slam," p. 56.
88. Quoted in Pattison, "Pinning Jesse Down," p. 92+.
89. Quoted in Tapper, *Body Slam*, p. 133.
90. Quoted in *A&E Biography*, "Body Slam Week: Jesse Ventura, The Body Politic."
91. Quoted in William Swanson, "Today The Governor's Office. Tomorrow The Beach?" *Minneapolis-St. Paul Magazine*, December 1999,. p. 86+.
92. Quoted in Pierce, "The First Hundred Hours," p. 103.
93. Quoted in Allen, *The Wit and Wisdom of Jesse "The Body . . . The Mind" Ventura*, p. ix.
94. Quoted in *A&E Biography*, "Body Slam Week: Jesse Ventura, The Body Politic."
95. Quoted in *A&E Biography*, "Body Slam Week: Jesse Ventura, The Body Politic."
96. Quoted in Pattison, "Pinning Jesse Down," p. 92+.

Chapter 6: Jesse "The Governor" Ventura

97. Quoted in O'Malley, "The Reluctant First Lady," p. 63.
98. Quoted in Bai and Brauer, "Jesse Ventura's 'Body' Politics," p. 41.
99. Ventura, *I Ain't Got Time to Bleed*, p. 45.
100. Quoted in Neal Karlen, "Governor Headlock," *Life*, March 1, 1999, p. 56+.
101. Quoted in Ventura inaugural speech, Minnesota State Government website.
102. Quoted in Pierce, "The First Hundred Hours," p. 102.
103. Quoted in *Hardball College Tour with Chris Matthews*, MSNBC, aired March 15, 2000.
104. Quoted in Conrad deFiebre, "Ventura Adds a Chapter—and Verse—to 'Bleed'," Minneapolis *Star Tribune*, May 25, 2000, front page.
105. Quoted in Scott S. Smith, "Wrestling with REFORM," *Entrepreneur*, January 2000, p. 97+.
106. Quoted in Charles Mahtesian, "Can He Govern?" *Governing*, May 2000.
107. Quoted in telephone interview with Ashley Grant of Associated Press, June 8, 2000.

108. Quoted in Bai and Brauer, "Jesse Ventura's 'Body' Politics," p. 41.
109. Quoted in Grobel, "Playboy Interview: Jesse Ventura," p. 55+.
110. Quoted in Neal Justin, "The Son Also Rises," Minneapolis *Star Tribune*, June 4, 2000, front page.
111. Quoted in Leiby, "I'm Not Like Other First Ladies," p. 29+.
112. Quoted in Bill Hewitt, "Power Politics" *People*, May 31, 1999, p. 126.
113. Quoted in Allen, *The Wit and Wisdom of Jesse "The Body . . . The Mind" Ventura*, p. 21.
114. Quoted in Bai and Brauer, "Jesse Ventura's 'Body' Politics," p. 38.
115. Quoted in John Rosengren, "Jesse the Brand," *Corporate Report-Minnesota*, November 1999, p. 18+.
116. Quoted in Ventura Files. www.venturafiles.com.
117. Quoted in Bai and Brauer, "Jesse Ventura's 'Body' Politics," p. 38.
118. Quoted in Hewitt, "Power Politics," p. 126.
119. Quoted in Justin, "The Son Also Rises," Minneapolis *Star Tribune*, front page.
120. Quoted in *Today*, Matt Lauer interviews Gov. Jesse Ventura, NBC, June 2, 1999.
121. Quoted in "The 25 Most Intriguing People of '99: Jesse Ventura," *People*, December 31, 1999, p. 58.
122. Quoted in Hewitt, "Power Politics," p. 126.
123. Quoted in Smith, "Wrestling with REFORM," p. 97+.
124. Quoted in telephone interview with Grant of Associated Press, June 8, 2000.
125. Quoted in telephone interview with Grant of Associated Press, June 8, 2000.

Epilogue: Jesse "The President" Ventura?

126. Quoted in Rosengren, "Jesse the Brand," p. 18+.
127. Kenneth T. Walsh, "A New Governor Hellbent On Innovative Politics," *U.S. News & World Report*, December 28, 1998, p. 69+.

128. Quoted in Matt Bai, "Wrestling For The Center," *Newsweek*, June 5, 2000, p. 32.
129. Quoted in Matt Bai, "Now He's the Man to See," *Newsweek*, October 11, 1999, p. 36+.
130. Quoted in Bai, "Wrestling For The Center," p. 33.
131. Quoted in Bob von Sternberg, "In His Own Words: Ventura on the Presidency," Minneapolis *Star Tribune*, June 1, 2000, Nation/World, front page.
132. Quoted in Rosengren, "Jesse the Brand," p. 18+.
133. Quoted in Pattison, "Pinning Jesse Down," p. 92+.
134. Quoted in Swanson, "Today The Governor's Office. Tomorrow The Beach?" p. 86+.
135. Quoted in Swanson, "Today The Governor's Office. Tomorrow The Beach?" p. 86+.

Important Dates in the Life of Jesse Ventura

1951
James George Janos is born July 15.

1969
In June, Janos graduates from Roosevelt High School.

1970
January 5, he leaves for basic training; completes SEAL training and begins the first of two tours of duty in Southeast Asia during the Vietnam War.

1973
In December Janos is discharged from the Navy and decides to live in California.

1974
Ventura returns to Minneapolis and in the spring enrolls in a community college, dropping out after one year to become a wrestler.

1975
He and Teresa Masters are married July 18 (a son, Tyrel, is born in 1979, and daughter, Jade, in 1983); on October 17, Ventura beats Jimmy "Superfly" Snuka for the Pacific Northwest heavyweight championship.

1979
Ventura joins the American Wrestling Association (AWA).

1980
On July 20, Ventura teams with Adrian "Golden Boy" Adonis to win the AWA tag team championship.

1984

Ventura retires from wrestling and becomes a ring announcer and actor.

1987

Ventura stars with Arnold Schwarzenegger in *Predator* to begin his film career.

1990

Ventura is elected mayor of Brooklyn Park, a Minneapolis suburb that is Minnesota's sixth largest city; he serves as mayor until 1995.

1998

On November 3, Ventura is elected governor.

1999

On January 4, Ventura is sworn in as Minnesota's 38th governor.

2000

On February 11, Ventura quits the Reform Party and helps re-establish the Independence Party of Minnesota.

For Further Reading

Keith Elliot Greenberg, *Biography: Jesse Ventura.* Minneapolis, MN: Lerner Publications Company, 2000. A solid, easy to read biography for the younger reader.

Jesse Ventura, *I Ain't Got Time to Bleed: Reworking the Body Politic From the Bottom Up.* New York: Villard, 1999. Ventura explains his political philosophy while recounting his life story.

Works Consulted

Books

Jessica Allen, *The Wit and Wisdom of Jesse "The Body . . . The Mind" Ventura.* New York: William Morrow and Company, Inc., 1999. Quotations from Ventura arranged by subject, such as his personal life, politics, and so forth.

Kevin Dockery and Bill Fawcett, *The Teams: An Oral History of the U.S. Navy SEALs.* New York: William Morrow and Company, Inc., 1998. Interviews with Ventura and other SEALs on their experiences within this elite military organization.

J. David Gillespie, *Politics at the Periphery: Third Parties in Two-Party America.* Columbia: University of South Carolina Press, 1993. A detailed look at how minor political parties have fared in U.S. political history.

Jake Tapper, *Body Slam: The Jesse Ventura Story.* New York: St. Martin's Paperbacks, 1999. A solid biography that explains the basic facts of Ventura's life through his election as Minnesota governor.

Periodicals

Matt Bai, "Now He's the Man to See," *Newsweek*, October 11, 1999, p. 36+.

Matt Bai, "Wrestling For The Center," *Newsweek*, June 5, 2000, pp. 32–33.

Matt Bai and David Brauer, "Jesse Ventura's 'Body' Politics," *Newsweek*, November 16, 1998, pp. 38–42.

Matthew Cooper, "Keeping His Eye on The Ball," *Time*, December 27, 1999, p. 128.

Works Consulted

Gidget Fuentes, "Former Sailor Ventura Takes Officers; Salutes," *Navy Times*, August 16, 1999, p. 13.

Paul Gray, "Body Slam," *Time*, November 16, 1998, pp. 54–57.

Lawrence Grobel, "Playboy Interview: Jesse Ventura." *Playboy*, November 1999, p. 55+.

Bill Hewitt, "Power Politics," *People*, May 31, 1999, pp. 124–26.

"Jesse Ventura," *Current Biography*, May 1999, pp. 52–56.

Neal Karlen, "Governor Headlock," *Life*, March 1, 1999, p. 56+.

Richard Leiby, "I'm Not Like Other First Ladies." *Good Housekeeping*, August, 1999, p. 29+.

Charles Mahtesian, "Can He Govern?" *Governing*, May 2000.

Kathy O'Malley, "The Reluctant First Lady," *McCall's*, July 1999, pp. 62–64.

Richard J. Newman and Rick Rickman, "Tougher Than Hell," *U.S. News & World Report*, November 3, 1997, p. 42+.

Kermit Pattison, "Pinning Jesse Down," *George*, March 1999, p. 92+.

Charles P. Pierce, "The First Hundred Hours," *Esquire*, April 1999, pp. 100–105.

John Rosengren, "Jesse the Brand," *Corporate Report–Minnesota*, November 1999, p. 18+.

Scott S. Smith, "Wrestling with REFORM," *Entrepreneur*, January 2000, p. 97+.

William Swanson, "Today The Governor's Office. Tomorrow The Beach?" *Minneapolis-St. Paul Magazine*, December 1999, p. 86+.

"The 25 Most Intriguing People of '99," *People*, December 31, 1999, p. 58.

Kenneth T. Walsh, "A New Governor Hellbent On Innovative Politics," *U.S. News & World Report*, December 28, 1998, p. 69+.

Newspapers

Conrad deFiebre, "Ventura Adds a Chapter—and Verse—to 'Bleed'," Minneapolis *Star Tribune*, May 25, 2000, front page.

Roger Ebert, "The Running Man," *Chicago Sun-Times*, November 13, 1987.

Neal Justin, "The Son Also Rises," Minneapolis *Star Tribune*, June 4, 2000, front page.

Britt Robson, "The Body Politic," *City Pages*, September 30, 1998.

Jake Tapper, "Barbarian at the Gate; Jesse Ventura's Rise to Power Parallels the Rise of Pro Wrestling," *Washington Post*, May 9, 1999, p. W16.

Bob von Sternberg, "In His Own Words: Ventura on the Presidency," Minneapolis *Star Tribune*, June 1, 2000, Nation/World, front page.

Television Shows

A&E Biography, "Body Slam Week: Jesse Ventura, The Body Politic," A&E, aired Nov. 18, 1999. Sixty minutes. A biography of Jesse Ventura that includes film clips of his life and interviews with friends, family members, and others.

Hardball College Tour with Chris Matthews, MSNBC, aired March 15, 2000. Sixty minutes. An interview with Jesse Ventura conducted at Winona State University in Minnesota.

Today, Matt Lauer interviews Gov. Jesse Ventura, NBC, June 2, 1999.

Internet

Letter by Jesse Ventura announcing he would quit the Reform Party. February 1, 2000. www.jesseventura.org/friendsofjv/frndltr.htm.

Review of *Abraxas, Guardian of the Universe,* Amazing World of Cult Movies Internet site, www.awcm.com.

Transcript of Internet interview conducted May 27, 1999, on the Barnes & Noble website, shop.barnesandnoble.com.

Ventura Files, a collection of Jesse Ventura facts and quotes compiled in one website, www.venturafiles.com.

Interview

Telephone interview by Ashley Grant of Associated Press, June 8, 2000.

Index

abortion rights, 75
Abraxas, Guardian of the Universe (movie), 54, 55
acting career
  college debut, 26
  first experience at, 16
  first role, 50
  interference with job as mayor, 64
  see also individual plays and movies
action figure, 9
  sales of, 82, 91
Adonis, Adrian "Golden Boy," 39
alcohol, 18, 31–32, 43,
American Wrestling Association (AWA), 37, 39
Arbogast, Grace, 62, 66
athletics, 16, 22
Atlas, Omar, 38

Barkley, Dean, 67
Basic Underwater Demolition/SEAL (BUD/S). *See* Hell Week
Batman and Robin (movie), 54
Belushi, Jim, 54
The Birds (play), 36
Bjorson, Ricky, 15
Bloom, Barry, 50
"The Body," 6, 9, 34–47
  copyrighting of, 57
Body Slam: The Jesse Ventura Story (Tapper), 15
"The Brand," 57, 82–83
Bransfield, Marjorie, 54
Brooklyn Park, Minnesota, 59–61
Brown, Jim, 53
Buck, Kathy, 17

campaign, 69–72
Capitol Wrestling Corporation, 45

Captain Freedom (movie character), 54
Carleton College, 71, 85
Carlson, Arne, 67
Champlin Park High School, 68
chewing tobacco, 64
childhood,
  athletics during, 14
  friends during, 15
  wild behavior during, 18–19
Coleman, Norm, 69, 72
Columbine High School, 85
Cooper Elementary School, 10
Coronado Naval Amphibious Base, 25, 27, 78

Davis, Don, 63
Deckerhoff, Gene, 55
Delano, Tom, 15, 16
Democratic–Farmer-Labor Party, 69
Democratic Party, 6, 69, 74
drugs, 43
Dyer, Bruce, 29

Ebert, Roger, 53
education, 76
  funding for, 76
  Ventura's graduation from high school, 24
employment
  as bodyguard for Rolling Stones, 7, 35
  as bouncer, 36
  in state highway department, 24
Enge, Joe, 60, 62
Engh, Rick, 64
Engstrom, Dolphin, 70
environmental issues, 20, 59, 62
Equal Rights Amendment, 61

family, 8–9, 78–81

fiscal policy, 75
Flatgard, Jerry, 15
football, 33
  as a coach, 68
  color commentator for, 55–56
  as player
    for Brooklyn Community College, 35–36
    at Roosevelt High School, 16–17
Fort Snelling National Cemetery, 8
Fox, Arnold, 50
Franklin (pet dog), 81
Frogmen, The (movie), 22–23

Gagne, Vern, 37, 39, 45, 46
gangs, 18–19
gay rights, 75
Geigel, Bob, 38
Gore, Al, 89, 90
Gotch, Frank, 37
Graham, Billy (wrestler), 37
Grant, Ashley, 77–78, 88
grass-roots politics, 71
Great Depression, 14
guerrilla warfare, 30
gun control, 84, 85

Hell Week, 26–27
Hercules, 36
Hermann, Tim, 68
Hogan, Hulk, 9, 46, 71
  championship fight with, 47
  No Holds Barred and, 54
  rivalry with, 40
  WCW and, 66
Huffman, Dave, 55
Humphrey, Hubert, 69
Humphrey, Hubert III, 69–70, 72
Hunter (TV show), 50

I Ain't Got Time to Bleed (Ventura), 52, 82
  about carousing overseas, 31–33
  on childhood, 18
  on the media, 87–88
  racial remarks made in, 84
Independence Party, 81
individual responsibility, 75
International Wrestling Institute and Museum (Newton, Iowa), 37

Jade Foundation, 80
Janos, Bernice Lenz (mother), 8, 11, 12
Janos, George (father), 8
  from Czechoslovakia, 12
  jobs held by, 14

World War II and, 11 12–13
Janos, Jade (daughter), 9
  birth of, 43
  epilepsy and, 43–44
  media distance from, 80
Janos, James George. *See* Ventura, Jesse
Janos, Jan (brother), 8–9, 10
  childhood of, 10, 15
  influence on brother, 21–22
  as Janos "the Clean," 29
  as swimmer, 16
Janos, Tyrel (son), 9
  birth of, 43
  as director, 79–80
Jennings, Dave, 76
"Jesse checks," 76
Jesse Ventura Show, The (radio), 56–57
Johnson, Kevin, 15

Kansas City, Missouri, 38, 41
Keck, Al, 55
Kennedy, John F., 56
KFAN-FM (radio station), 55
Krautkremer, Jim, 60, 61
KSTP (radio station), 66
KSTP-FM (radio station), 56

Lake Nokomis, 20
Late Night with David Letterman (TV show), 84
Lee, Damian, 54
Levitan, Jerry, 54
Lightstone, Marilyn, 54

Maple Grove, 64, 65
Masters, Teresa. *See* Ventura, Terry
Mayne Moondog, 39
McCain, John, 89
McInroy, Freeman "Mac," 19
McMahon, Vince, Jr., 45, 48
media, 84
military service, 29–30, 84
  refusal to talk about, 29
  nicknamed "the Dirty" during, 22
  see also Vietnam War
Milwaukee Lutheran Hospital, 12
Minneapolis, Minnesota, 7, 35, 39, 55,
Minnesota Timberwolves, 86–87
Minnesota Vikings, 55
Minnesota Legislature, 76–78
Mitchell, Frances, 54
Mongols, 34–35
Motivation Week. *See* Hell Week
Moy, Terry "Mother," 32

Index

National Wrestling Alliance, 38
Navy. U.S., 7, 9, 26
  see also SEALs
Nelson, Steve, 10, 23, 35
Nicholson, Jack, 79
No Holds Barred (movie), 54
Northern Illinois University, 24
North Hennepin Community College, 25–36

Okerlund, "Mean Gene," 48
Olsen, David Bradley, 92
Orfield, Myron, 57

Pacific Northwest Heavy Weight Championship, 30
patriotism, 9
Patton, George, 11
Pawlenty, Tim, 87–88
Pearl Harbor, 12
Penn, Sean, 79–80
Piper, "Rowdy" Roddy, 50
Playboy interview, 84–85
politics, 19, 59
  in high school studies, 9
  Lake Nokomis and, 20
  parents' views on, 20–21
Predator (movie), 50–51, 58
presidency, 89–93
Professor Toru, 53
Pure Ventura (radio show), 57

Quie, Al, 74

racism, 49–50, 84
radio, 54–57, 66
Rather, Dan, 6
Reform Party, 6
  campaign finance and term limits and, 67
  Ventura's leaving of, 81
  struggles of candidate in, 69–70
religion, 85
Remagen Bridge, 12
Republican Party, 6, 69, 74
Roberts Rules of Order, 62
Rockwood, Harvey, 65
Rolling Stones, 7, 35
Roosevelt High School, 16, 24
Rowe, Dan, 55
Running Man, The (movie), 53
Rusty Nail, 36, 41

Sanford Middle School, 16
Saturday Night Main Events (TV show), 50

Schier, Steven, 71, 85
Schwarzenegger, Arnold, 53
  acting with, 50
  training with, 52
scuba diving, 22
SEALs (Sea-Air-Land), 6, 22–23
  early training in, 25
  factors for joining, 22
  football in, 30
  Hell Week, 26–27
  history of, 24
  influence on life, 32
  Jan's entry into, 21
  physical training in, 30, 32
SERE (Survival, Escape, Resistance, and Evasion), 27, 29
Sergeant Blain (movie character), 52
Seventh Street Gym, 37
sex, 43
Sharkey, Eddie, 37
Sharp Cabrillo Hospital (San Diego), 47
Snuka, Jimmy "Superfly," 39
social issues, 74
  conservation concerns, 20
  Equal Rights Amendment, 61
  gay rights, 75
  legalizing prostitution, 84
"South Side Boys," 18, 19
Spark, Paul, 31
Spong, Doug, 82
Stanford Middle School, 19
St. Paul, 7
St. Paul Civic Center, 41
Stromberg, Robert, 64, 65–66
Subic Bay (Philippine Islands), 29
SummerSlam (pay-per-view event), 50
swimming, 16, 22
  failure to get scholarship in, 24, 25
  in Mississippi River, 15

Tag Team (TV pilot), 50
Tampa Bay Buccaneers, 54–55
Tapper, Jake, 37, 46
Target Center, 74
taxes, 59, 62–63, 75–76
The Teams: An Oral History of the U.S. Navy SEALS (Dockery and Fawcett), 24
Throsen, Sven-Ole, 52, 54
Thunderground (movie), 79
Timothy Evangelical Lutheran Church, 41
Titan, 58
Turner, Ted, 66
Twin Cities, 7, 59

Underwater Demolition Team 12 (UDT), 29
unicameral legislature, 78

Van Lidth, Erland, 53
Ventura, Jesse
  academic ability of, 19–20, 24
  advice to presidential candidate, 90–91
  as announcer
    prompted by illness to become an, 47
    racist remarks as, 49–50
    in the ring, 48, 66
  birth of, 7
  blood clot ends career of, 47
  as capitalist, 82
  clothing worn by, 61–62
  colorblindness of, 25–26
  distrust of politicians by, 67
  future of, 93
  as governor
    campaign for, 69–72
    commitment to family, 81
    controversial remarks of, 84–86
    failures of, 78, 62
    humanistic style of, 74–76
    making money during term, 82–83
    problems with the legislature, 76–78
    straight talk on issues and, 70
    successes of, 87–88
    tax rebates and, 75–76
  intimidating personal style of, 54
  as "Janos the Dirty," 29
  marriage of, 41, 43
  as mayor
    absenteeism of, 64
    attempts to reduce taxes by, 62, 63
    decision to run and, 62
    residency controversy and, 65, 66
    successes of, 63
  picking the name of, 34
  as popular student, 17
  private life of, 43
  self-promotion of, 91–93
  wrestling style of, 40

Ventura, Terry, 6
  on Brooklyn Park issues, 60–61
  on being first lady, 80
  first date with, 42
  marriage, 41
  meeting of, 36
Ventura for Minnesota, Inc., 82
Vietnam War, 7
  frogman during, 23
  influence on politics views, 20
  Jan's service in, 23
  support of movement to end draft, 61
  types of SEAL missions during, 30
  war veterans of, 9

Ware, Koko B., 49
Widmark, Richard, 22
The Wit and Wisdom of Jesse "The Body". . . "The Mind" Ventura (Allen), 62
Wichita, Kansas, 38
World Championship Wrestling, 68
World Wrestling Federation (WWF)
  as guest announcer during gubernatorial term, 82
  joining, 45–46
  lawsuit against, 58
WrestleMania IV (TV special), 50
wrestling, 6, 33, 57–58
  attempt to start a union for, 61
  babyface (good guy) in, 38
  backbreaker move, 40
  championship match, 30
  first experience at, 16
  as heel (bad guy) in, 38
  history of, 37
  style of, 40
  turning pro, 36–38

X-Files, The (TV show), 50

The Young and the Restless (TV show)
  appearance on, 92

Zevon, Warren, 74

Picture Credits

Cover photo: © Malcolm Mackinnon/Retna Ltd.
© AFP/Corbis, 60, 65
Archive Photos, 11
Pierre Aslan/F. Nebinger/D. Nivière/Sipa Press, 79
Nina Berman/Sipa Press, 77, 80
Clark Campbell/Sipa Press, 86
Classmates.com Yearbook Archives, 17
Scott Cohen/Sipa Press, 7, 68, 72
National Archives, 20
Photofest, 23, 40, 49, 51, 53, 75
Reuters/Scott Cohen/Archive Photos, 8, 69, 92
Reuters/Eric Miller/Archive Photos, 42, 44, 56, 83, 90
© Michael Siluk, 15
Sipa Press, 27, 31
© Ronnie Wright/Corbis, 45
Earl Young/Archive Photos, 28

About the Author

Michael V. Uschan has written a dozen books, including *America's Founders*, a multiple biography of George Washington, Thomas Jefferson, and other early U.S. leaders, and *The Importance of John F. Kennedy*, both for Lucent Books. Mr. Uschan began his career as a writer and editor with United Press International, a wire service that provided stories to newspapers, radio, and television. Journalism is sometimes called "history in a hurry," and Mr. Uschan considers writing history books a natural extension of skills he developed in his many years as a working journalist. He and his wife, Barbara, live in the Milwaukee suburb of Franklin, Wisconsin.